What others are saying

The history of one of the world's most majestic sports, harness racing, is well over 200 years old in the United States and, one of the most iconic facilities encompassing harness racing's grand tradition, Roosevelt Raceway, is brought to life in a most succinct manner by authors Victoria M. Howard, Billy Haughton and Freddie Hudson.

Now closed for more than a quarter century, Roosevelt Raceway is where night time harness racing began and flourished for some four plus decades.

The authors have unlocked a vault of memories, not only reliving history under the lights as many of today's "old-timers" witnessed, but unearthing occurrences that, heretofore, were kept "hushed up"—only known by a few raceway executives—now erased from this earth, either naturally or otherwise, and a few underworld cronies, also no longer in this world, again, either naturally or otherwise.

The initial chapters deal with George Morton Levy, the founding father of racing under the stars, and his connections with the underworld and politicians, some of whom were as crooked as many of the numbers on the Roosevelt Raceway infield tote-board.

The book also covers the introduction of the "savior" of the sport—the mobile starting gate—as well as the celebrities, fatal occurrences, riots and characters that made Roosevelt Raceway the subject matter in, literally, millions of conversations over the years.

Great horses, like the artichoke eating French bred trotter Jamin and the grand Su Mac Lad, who, literally, wore out three sets of "free-for-all" trotters over his career, are brought back to life in this book...as well as greats like Bye Bye Byrd, Adios Butler, Cardigan Bay and Bret Hanover.

And, of course, the book completes its task with a tribute to many of the sport's great drivers who competed at Roosevelt Raceway—Billy, Stanley, Buddy, "Loosh," "The Red Man," Herve, Benny "The Whip" and "Toothpick Del," to name a few.

One of my favorite chapters is the one entitled "Stories Remembered," a hilarious recollection of anecdotes both on and off the track.

This book is a "must" for racing fans. It will bring back great memories and lighten every day it is in your hands.

—John Berry
Communicators Hall of Fame Journalist

ROOSEVELT RACEWAY

Where It All Began

ROOSEVELT RACEWAY

Where It All Began

Victoria M. Howard · Freddie Hudson · Billy Haughton

TATE PUBLISHING
AND ENTERPRISES, LLC

Published by Tate Publishing & Enterprises, LLC
127 E. Trade Center Terrace | Mustang, Oklahoma 73064 USA
1.888.361.9473 | www.tatepublishing.com

Tate Publishing is committed to excellence in the publishing industry. The company reflects the philosophy established by the founders, based on Psalm 68:11,
"The Lord gave the word and great was the company of those who published it."

Book design copyright © 2014 by Tate Publishing, LLC. All rights reserved.
Cover design by Kathy Estes and Joana Quilantang
Interior design by Honeylette Pino
Editing by John Berry

Published in the United States of America

ISBN: 978-1-63418-422-9
1. Sports & Recreation / Horse Racing
2. Architecture / Buildings / Landmarks & Monuments
14.10.08

To all the people that I have met while
being involved in the sport of harness racing. A special thanks
to John Berry- Communicators Hall of Fame journalist-
for his much appreciated help in editing this book. Also, to two
of my "favorite" trainers, Bruce Nickells and Mel Turcotte, for
giving me the most memorable and exciting
times in this wonderful sport.

—Victoria M. Howard

To the celebration of a great time in the history
of harness racing.So many people were able to spend their lives
and friendships in a unique and popular environment known
as Roosevelt Raceway. The track and its surroundings left them
with wonderful memories for so many years.
I am blessed to have been part of it.

—Billy Haughton

To the drivers, trainers, owners, grooms, horses,
and all the employees of Roosevelt Raceway; and especially to
the fans, because without them, we would not be writing this
book. A special thanks to Steve Dunkel, the former paddock
judge at Roosevelt Raceway, who motivated and supported
me in writing this book. He unfortunately
passed away before its publication.

—Freddie Hudson

Contents

Book Two

Preface

Roosevelt Raceway: Where It All Began was written to recapture the undying excitement, confirm the facts, and relive the history of the one and only Roosevelt Raceway. The book begins with the initial opening in 1940 as it retraces those memorable and exciting times.

As you read this book, you will experience what it felt like to stand in the winner's circle, the highs and the lows that harness racing brought to millions, and the heartbreak that was felt by saying good-bye to the end of this legacy in 1988.

The book personally introduces you to the founders, drivers, trainers, and world-class horses that made Roosevelt undoubtedly, one of the best harness tracks of all times. It was not only written for trainers, drivers, and owners of racehorses, but for *anyone* and *everyone* who embraces the passion and love for the sport of harness racing and that incredible creature called the *horse*. It was also written for those people who were lucky enough to have been a part of Roosevelt Raceway and the history that occurred there.

This book is for everyone: Young and old, horsemen and gamblers, or for those who just wish to discover the exciting world of harness racing and how it was transformed from a county fair sport to a major league sport. This book will appeal to people from all walks of life for it has something in it for everyone to enjoy. It contains history, facts, original pictures, and stories about the number one harness racetrack in the world. The authentic photos that are displayed in this book are priceless.

Roosevelt Raceway: Where It All Began consists of two separate books within one binding. The first part is Book One, which explains how harness racing began, the continent's first organized sport. It tells about the life and times of George Levy, the father of harness racing and the founder of Roosevelt Raceway.

Book Two contains information about the drivers, world-class horses, and the famous races that called Roosevelt Raceway "home." Roosevelt Raceway was a landmark to the residents of Long Island as the Tower of Pisa is to Italy and Big Ben is to England. It was the heart and soul of the Big Apple.

The authors of this book are three passionate people who together have 150 years combined experience in various aspects of this sport. Two of the authors grew up in the harness horse business with fathers who were legends. They knew firsthand what it was like to experience the thrills and heartaches the sport brought. The third author, Victoria Howard, has owned, trained, and bred harness horses for over forty years. When these three advocates of harness racing discovered there had never been a single book written about this historical racetrack, they decided to collaborate and write one to help resurrect Roosevelt Raceway—even if only on paper—for they have personally felt, and still feel, the passion of this exciting sport.

Their wish and goal is that in writing this book, although harness racing may never be at the level it once was, it may help bring it a little closer. The factual stories of the drivers, owners, and horses that made Roosevelt Raceway the controversial and legendary track it was—and always will be—are revealed within these pages.

Note: The contents and information in this book is not necessarily that of the authors, but was obtained from research, information, interviews, and facts known to be accurate. The authors are not responsible or liable for any information that may be incorrect. (All information, interviews, testimonials, and stories used in this book were given permission to be printed or reproduced.)

Introduction

For those people who have never heard of Roosevelt Raceway, this book was written to inform and enlighten them on the times that took place at this famous harness racetrack. Although the track has been closed for over twenty-five years, the history that was made there during the half century it was opened and running is everlasting.

Interesting Facts about R.R.

Roosevelt Raceway was built on what was called Roosevelt Field #1—the "upper" field—which was the site of Charles Lindbergh's 1927 solo transatlantic flight. It was on this same field that Amelia Earhart and Wiley Post made history. The field (and the future harness track Roosevelt Raceway) was named after Quentin Roosevelt—an aviation pilot. Quentin was the son of former president Teddy Roosevelt, and was killed in action when his plane was shot down in Germany during World War I.

Roosevelt Raceway was the very first track in the nation to run an extended evening harness meet under the lights. It was the original home of the Messenger Stakes, part of the "Triple Crown of Harness Racing for Pacers." It was also the track which founded and raced the famous "International Trot," and hosted the event until the track closed in 1988.

Prior to Roosevelt becoming the most popular harness track in the country, night racing had been an occasional spectacle at fairs, and only a dream.

Roosevelt Raceway was known as the "Taj Mahal" of harness racing. The track officially opened its doors on September 2, 1940, and sadly closed them almost a half century later on June 15, 1988. Before becoming the "World Capital of Harness Racing," the site was part of the Hempstead Plains, which was located in an unincorporated area of the Town of Hempstead.

Prior to it becoming one of the most famous racetracks in the nation, a great deal of history took place there. In the days of the First World War, the field had been known as Hazlehurst Field, where the likes of aviation hopefuls such as Jimmy Doolittle and Gene Barksdale trained.

In 1936, an auto racetrack was built there to host the Vanderbilt Cup. Two decades later, in 1956, Roosevelt Raceway was noted as being the first racetrack that would be accepted by the American Stock Exchange.

The Rise and Fall of RR

Roosevelt Raceway was originally leased in 1939 by a group of businessmen and investors called the Old Country Trotting Association. The "brains" behind this venture was a lawyer named George Morton Levy. He became internationally renowned as the "Father of the Modern Harness Racing Industry" and the "Pioneer of Nighttime Racing."

During the years that Roosevelt was operating, many track and world records were set there. Multiple scandals surfaced which brought much publicity to the track. Many known as well as several unknown drivers who called

Roosevelt home would make history and have their names inscribed in the history books.

ಬಂಞ

So what caused this prominent racetrack, the place millions of people loved and attended, to close its doors forever? After Levy, died in 1977, the empire which he had built started to collapse. It's speculated that, in 1971, the introduction of "Off Track Betting," which first started in New York, was one of the main causes for the decline in attendance at all of the States' racetracks. Also during that time, commercial growth and change outside the raceways diverted people to other interests.

On September 1, 1976, a new harness racetrack opened in New Jersey called The Meadowlands, which quickly became a solid competitor for Roosevelt. Today, little remains of what was once the hottest racetrack in the nation. Sadly, the site of the grandstand and track (which remained vacant for years) is now the home of a luxury condominium complex called the "Meadowbrook Commons," and the area which once housed some of the best racehorses in the world is now a hardware store.

Through this book, the authors hope to resurrect those days and help memorialize the passion, excitement, and history that this incredible racetrack provided to millions.

Enjoy!

Book 1

The Story

Part I

Early Roosevelt Raceway, Clint Hodgins & Texas Hanover

George Morton Levy, the founder of Roosevelt Raceway

Roosevelt Raceway paddock 1941

1

Where It All Began

"If It Moves, They Will Bet On It."

—George Morton Levy

George Morton Levy,
the Father of Harness Racing

Before we begin telling the story of how one of the most famous harness tracks in the world came to be, we must introduce the founder of Roosevelt Raceway. If it wasn't for this man, Roosevelt Raceway would not have been created, and harness racing would not have grown to be the popular sport that it came to be. He influenced so many people in this industry and helped pave the way to what would become one of the most exciting sports in the world: harness racing.

The man we are talking about is George Morton Levy. He was born in 1888 in the south shore village of Seaford, Long Island. While studying at New York University (from which he graduated cum laude), he learned how to make a dollar, the art of diplomacy, and legal maneuvering. Levy not only became a successful criminal lawyer, but he was a genius who had a vision of turning a hobby sport into a legacy millions of people worldwide would enjoy. His friends and colleagues were a colorful bunch, in both his personal and business life, for he never judged anyone and treated people equally. One of Levy's friends and golf partner was a man named Frank Costello, who was a leading underworld figure of whom he was often criticized for his friendship. When asked about his alliance with Costello, he would say, "It's not *who* you defend, it's *how* you defend." The two men met in the 1930s and quickly became friends.

In the early 1930s, George Morton Levy's son, George Morton Levy Jr., was involved in an accident that left him partially paralyzed from the waist down. Levy was overwhelmed with medical bills and was not sure how he would pay them. One day in court, Frank Costello came up to Levy and handed him an envelope that contained $2,500, which was well needed. Levy accepted the money, paid off his son's medical bills, and paid back the entire loan to Costello within two weeks.

But probably Levy's most infamous client and friend was a man known worldwide. His name was Charles Luciano. Luciano, who ultimately was nicknamed "Lucky," was known as the "Father of Modernized Crime in the United States."

In 1936, Levy represented Luciano when he was charged with compulsory prostitution and slavery. Although the brilliant lawyer won most of his cases, in this case, he did not. Luciano was found guilty and sentenced thirty to fifty years in prison. This case was a paradox, for it proved no matter how much money a crime boss has made, or how well his lawyer represents him, he still can be convicted and sent to prison. But even after the sentence was passed, the persistent Levy continued to fight for his client. Nine years later, Luciano was released from prison and deported to Italy.

He got the name "Lucky" because he won many crap games and had survived a severe beating and throat slitting.

It is said that Levy—through his notorious and colorful friends—learned how much money could be made in booking bets. In 1939, the state of New York legalized parimutuel wagering on horse racing. Knowing the ins and outs of illegal bookmaking, Levy, the genius, put his knowledge and experience to work to incorporate it into the legal parimutuel betting that would soon become available in the state of New York.

ഇൻരു

To the sport of harness racing, Levy brought a marketing and merchandising concept. He backed the development of the mobile starting gate which would revolutionize harness racing and put it on the map. Levy was able to establish single dash racing, as opposed to the heat system, due to the increase supply of racehorses. He paved the way for what would become one of the greatest sports in the world.

Although Levy was "tough as nails" when it came to business, he also had a seldom-seen tender side. He was lovingly called "the marrying man" by his friends, for as he was in business, he was also in his personal life (not afraid to take a chance.) The oft-wedded attorney, who was the guiding genius behind the fabulously successful Roosevelt Raceway, had, during his life, married three of his secretaries. When those relationships went sour, Levy took the plunge a fourth time with a pert, thirty-year-old pretty blonde named Elise Huelle (who had never taken dictation from Levy.) The smitten lovers had a two-year romance before sealing their vows at a Maryland farm which was owned by Levy's business partner, Alvin Weil. This would be Levy's final marriage, which would produce two children a son named Bobby, and a beautiful daughter, CeCe, who was the apple of her father's eye.

In 1965, Elise became very ill and was diagnosed with a rare disease called scleroderma. Immediately, Levy started seeking advice from the best professionals, and was willing to pay any amount of money to anyone who had a cure for this disease. After a two-year illness, in 1967, Elise Levy succumbed to her illness at the age of forty-nine. Subsequently, with the death of his wife, it was said that George Morton Levy was never the same.

ഇന്ദ

On October 15, 1966, Levy and Johnson sold their shares of stock of Roosevelt Raceway to the San Juan Racing Associates, which was led by Hyman Glickstein. Levy remained on board as chief counsel and chairman of the board at Roosevelt Raceway. Shortly afterward, Alvin Weil, Levy's other partner, resigned as president due to differences with track associates. With Weil's resignation, Levy added the job of president to his responsibilities. Up until his death in 1977, George Morton Levy passionately fought to keep Roosevelt Raceway alive and thriving. His passion for the sport was real and he had a sincere love for the horses and horsemen. After Levy's death, Roosevelt Raceway and the sport of harness racing began to disintegrate. Since that time harness racing has never been the same.

In The Beginning
1940

Finally, after many rain delays, the official opening day at Roosevelt Raceway was September 2, 1940. On this historic night, about five thousand people wagered $40,742, which was bet on the eight races that took place that evening. The mutual handle was considered "on the light side," due to the fact that many of the spectators knew little about the horses competing.

As Levy watched the near empty buses arriving on the dirt road which led to the grandstand, he was amazed at the many autos that were following the buses. Although the attendance that night was a little disappointing (for they had expected about fifteen thousand people), the Old Country Trotting Association, to whom the meet was licensed, declared the evening a success. This was the first time that night racing was ever held in the state of New York.

℘℘

In 1944, Roosevelt Raceway finally began to turn a profit and on June 8, 1946, Roosevelt Raceway saw its first $500,000 on track handle.

The ambiance of Roosevelt was distinctive. Sitting atop of the grandstand/clubhouse roof was a large illuminated sign. The course was set in front of the long row of stands that faced the stretch when the raceway was earlier used for automobile racing. Operating with the same floodlights that the midget cars had used, the horses could be seen as clearly as if watching them in daylight; the half-mile track was small enough so that the horses were never out of clear sight of the spectators. The paddock where the horses were kept before the races was conveniently located at the end of the first turn available for the patrons to amble around among the horses.

❦

Originally, post time for the first race was set at 8:00 p.m., but a large part of the crowd did not arrive until later. For that reason, the management announced that races for the following night would begin a half hour later, with a twenty-minute break between races.

While the field of six horses got in their assigned positions, the tension in the grandstands was so thick you could cut it with a knife. That race would be the first of many that would take place over the half-mile racetrack in the years ahead.

❦

Roosevelt Raceway offered 102 mutual windows: some designated for accepting money and others for paying money out. The track also offered the McNamara starting barrier. Unlike today, the barrier would allow drivers to pass the starter in the opposite direction of the race. After the drivers were twenty feet past him, he would call them to turn and line up in position. As the drivers and their horses approached, he would raise the barrier and start the race. If it was a fair clean start, the race would begin; if not, there would be a recall. During those days, there were many frustrating recalls, until the discovery of the starting gate in 1946.

❦

That evening, a lovely filly by the name of Martha Lee would cross the finish line first, with the colts in the race hopelessly pursuing her. The purse for that particular race was $250, which awarded the winner $125. Not bad for a night's work. Martha Lee, the winning horse, paid $4.40, $3.10, and $2.50, with driver John "Red" Hanafin in the sulky. Although the total money wagered that night was a disappointing $40,742, Levy and his associates could see the potential.

ॐ

The millions of people lucky enough to have attended Roosevelt Raceway experienced excitement, entertainment, and thrills beyond words. You could always feel electricity flowing through the air .The moans, groans, laughter, and the heart-pounding thrills were what made Roosevelt Raceway the legacy it was and always will be.

For the people who attended Roosevelt Raceway, there are certain things that they will never forget, such as:

- The windows lined with eager patrons hoping to wager their bets before the bell rang.
- The cop who stopped traffic for the horses competing in the races to cross the street.
- The man selling balloons to the patrons to bring home to their kids and the pretzel man selling those freshly baked pretzels.
- That distinct smell of hot dogs and knishes on the bottom floor grandstand.
- The "secret" $50 to $100 window designated strictly for the high rollers who wanted to remain anonymous.

- In the center of the lobby, the "Doc Robbins Program" booth which predicted the winners of each race.
- The excited patrons leaning on the rail watching the horses and drivers parade by.
- The excitement of the stretch drives as the drivers holding the lines with one hand and cracking their whips with the other yelling encouragement to their horses.

Some people remember one driver in particular, a man named Del Insko, who always had his "signature" toothpick hanging from his mouth. And of course, those who attended Roosevelt will never forget the distinctive sound of announcer Jack E. Lee, whose voice could be heard throughout the grounds as he called the races shouting, "And here comes Carmine on the extreme outside to take the lead."

> Roosevelt Raceway, it was ours from the beginning—
> we owned it—and it belonged to us.

Bringing Harness Racing to America

The origins of modern harness racing are indeed to be found in North America where trotting harness races became a popular rural hobby. These races were usually run in fairly unsophisticated carts and on pot, hole-riddled country roads. Trotting in North America also had its heritage in road racing, but it was in the early nineteenth century when many trotting tracks began popping up in the United States. The popularity of pacers initiated with the arriving of the Big Four in the United States (Mattie Hunter, Sleepy Tom, Rowdy Boy, and Lucy) during the

1870s. At that time, there were two other great race mares whose names were Goldsmith Maid and Nancy Hanks. The mare Nancy Hanks was named after her owner, Nancy, who was President Abe Lincoln's mother.

Also adding to the recognition was the coming of the "first two-minute harness horse" in 1897, a pacer named Star Pointer, and the overwhelming popularity of a horse named Dan Patch in the early years of the twentieth century. Dan Patch (1896–1916) was an outstanding pacer who broke world records at least fourteen times in the early 1900s. The legendary horse earned the title of being the "World's Champion Harness Horse" and the "Greatest Harness Horse in the History of the Two-Wheeled Sulky." Dan Patch was likely the first endorsed athlete who would set the way for future athletes (football, baseball, and basketball players) who would receive significant monies to endorse a product (e.g. Nike, Hanes, etc.). During his lifetime, Dan Patch endorsed over thirty products—sleds, coasters, wagons, tobacco, cigars, washing machines, toys, gasoline engines, stock feed, even a Dan Patch automobile. Dan Patch was treated like the royalty he was, for he even had his own private railroad car that he toured in! The horse was named for his original owner, Dan Messner, and his sire, Joe Patchen. In 1900, Messner sold the horse to Manley Sturgess for a record $20,000. In 1902, Sturgess sold Dan Patch to Marion Willis Savage of Minnesota, where the horse lived until he died at the age of twenty.

And we can't forget to mention a handsome, gray standardbred stallion named Greyhound. Greyhound was by Guy Abbey out of Elizabeth by Peter the Great. Born in 1932 Greyhound was the "Outstanding Trotting Horse" of his day and arguably the greatest in the history of the sport.

He was nicknamed by his fans the "Great Grey Ghost" and "Silver-Skinned Flyer." In 1935, Greyhound won the Hambletonian race, and in 1938 he lowered the record time for trotting to 1:55 1/4. That was a remarkable race time for those days. Greyhound's record would stand for thirty-one years. The "Silver-Skinned Flyer" also held the record for racing under saddle. After his death in 1965, Greyhound was rightfully honored as Horse of the Century.

℘℘

Before Roosevelt Raceway opened, most standardbred racing was performed by trotters. This was the track who promoted the pacer. Bettors soon found that pacers were generally faster than the trotters and enjoyed betting on them for they had a better chance of cashing a ticket. They thought that, because trotters broke often, their money was safer in betting on a pacer. One horseman at that time said, "The only way a trotter can beat a pacer is to start before him."

Important Changes

In the forties, two important changes occurred. First, there was the introduction of parimutuel racing under the lights. In the year 1940, Roosevelt Raceway was the very first track to execute this type of racing. Second was the institution of the "mobile starting gate," which was also instituted at Roosevelt Raceway in the year 1946. With these two important changes, the sport quickly surged.

By 1948, attendance tripled, state revenue increased nearly eightfold, purses nearly tenfold, and membership in the United States Trotting Association (founded in 1938 as a merger of other groups after the governance of harness racing had fallen into disarray) nearly quintupled. Now, a half century later, the sport of harness racing (although it has declined for many reasons) is still dearly loved and followed by millions worldwide.

Many thanks go to Roosevelt Raceway and founder George Morton Levy as the driving forces behind this exciting sport, for this was the racetrack, and the man, that put harness racing on the map and in history books.

Large Roosevelt crowd 1941

Bettors looking in the paddock 1948

Drivers getting rule instructions 1940's

2

The Birth of a Legacy

"Now I have friends. They're not from Palermo,
they're from Sicily. They're not even Italians. They're
Jewish. But they're still my friends and I trust 'em."

—Lucky Luciano

America in the Forties

The year was 1940. For the people living in America, hope
was on the horizon. The thirties had seen the worst drought
in American history, and the stock market crash provided
a dramatic end to an era of prosperity. During those days,
parimutuel gambling had just been legalized in the state
of New York. In 1939, notorious gangster Al Capone's
gang was operating the dog racing tracks in the country.
Licenses to conduct parimutuel gambling races in states
were restricted in number by law. It was then that effort
was being made to pass the 1939 bill, which took place
when Assemblyman Penny met with William H. Cane.
At that time, Assemblyman Cane had been running the

Hambletonian (the famous trotting race) for many years under the license of the Goshen Mile Track Association of New Jersey. Although there were mixed emotions about legalized gambling among the people, many saw this as a great opportunity to make money—and lots of it.

℘⃝

In 1938 and 1939, George Morton Levy represented the midget car track owners on illegal gambling in Roosevelt Raceway. When it was brought to the attention of the State Constitutional Committee that spectators at the midget auto races held at Roosevelt Raceway could purchase "certificates" of participation in purses awarded to the race winners, a hearing was called. It was said that those who held certificates on the winning cars would share the purses. A season's purse participation certificate would cost $200 less a discount, or an investor could make four monthly payments of $50 each month in the winning capacity of a car. A third option was that an investor could invest a $2 certificate share each day of the season.

℘⃝

During that time, Levy represented Lucky Luciano, Frank Costello, and Frank Erickson (one of the country's wealthiest bookmakers) and quickly saw the monetary value of racing and owning a racetrack. In 1935, Erickson had been indicted on charges of vagrancy and also of making false statements in applications for pistol permits. Acting as Erickson's attorney, Levy fought to have all charges dropped on his client. With the clientele Levy had represented, he soon discovered the ins and outs of the bookmaking business which would later prove to be beneficial while owning and operating Roosevelt Racetrack.

Granting of the Licenses

It all started in November 1939 when the voters of the state voted by referendum to legalize betting on horse races. The first licenses were granted in 1940 to conduct gambling harness meets. These were assigned to the Orange County Driving Park (which ran five days at Historic Half Mile Track, Goshen), Mr. Cane's New Jersey Association (which ran five days at a mile track in Goshen), the Genessee Monroe Racing Association (which ran thirty days at a fairground called Batavia Downs, Batavia), and the Old County Trotting Association (which held a thirty-day meet at Roosevelt Raceway, Westbury, Long Island).

₭⁗℄

Back in those days, harness racing was a small-fry operation confined in most part to state fairs and rural county tracks. At that time, the sport of harness racing was run at multiple places, including the Mineola Fair Grounds, with the races being conducted during the day. Unlike today, the purses for the races were put up by the drivers and trainers themselves who were competing against each other.

This was one of the main reasons why the future founders of Roosevelt (Levy and Johnson) thought they could be successful in this endeavor. But nothing good comes easy and it wasn't easy getting all the i's dotted and t's crossed. The first thing that had to be done was to form a racing commission to govern and grant racing dates. They tapped into the local upper society for support, which was well accepted.

₭⁗℄

Up until that time, harness racing was held during the daytime hours. Unfortunately, daytime racing caused a big problem for the majority of people who worked during the day. To correct this situation, the establishment decided to run racing at night, thus giving the patrons the opportunity to attend the races after work. Another reason they were pushing for nighttime racing was that they didn't want to compete with the thoroughbred racing which was held during the day. Once evening racing was approved, several prominent businessmen decided to open a half-mile track which would be called Roosevelt Raceway.

The genius of the Westbury track was the aforementioned George Morton Levy, a Mineola lawyer who originally started Old Country Trotting Association in 1940. Some people say he was a clairvoyant, because he foresaw what a prosperous and historical track **Roosevelt Raceway** could be. He proved them right. Along for the ride with Levy was a successful broker named Robert G. Johnson. The two men collaborated and opened the track with $25,000, which they had borrowed.

ℐℛ

Back in those days, most people were more interested in flat racing (thoroughbred) than in harness racing. George Levy was not one of them. As a child growing up in New York, George would regularly visit the nearby harness tracks where he would wager a few dollars amongst friends. Levy loved watching the beautiful horses race around the track and was quickly hooked on the sport. Never in his wildest dreams did this young boy from Seaford, New York, think that one day he would own one of the most famous racetracks in the world. Roosevelt Raceway would become known as "the home to world record holders," "the place where many scandals would occur" and it would be here that some of the best drivers, trainers, and horses would have their names etched in stone forever. Roosevelt Raceway was also known as a "Good Neighbor," for it contributed much to the economic health, growth, and cultural enrichment of the county.

80Q3

Because of the war, harness racing ceased for a year. When the war was over, racing resumed at Roosevelt Raceway with a bang! Although the official records are not exact (because they only counted paid admissions, and the track did not charge any of the military personnel that patronized the track), track attendance soared.

Being the benevolent man he was, George Morton Levy jumped right on the bandwagon, helping with the war efforts. During the meet, one week would be designated where all the monies brought in from betting and paid attendance would be donated to a war-based charity. Throughout the entire meet, all the monies that were made from parking (parking fee of $0.25) went directly to the USAF Aid Society. Due to gas rationing, Levy sent horse-drawn wagons to pick up fans at the train station.

In 1944, Roosevelt Raceway brought in $10,000,000 more than they did in 1941, and during the seventy-three days of racing, the total mutual handle was $15,078,831.

80Q3

In September, the New York state started an investigation into accusations of bribing politicians to pass the parimutuel horse racing bill in 1939. They were questioning a $10,000 loan that Roosevelt Raceway had made to Buffalo Raceway.

Shortly afterward, Levy and Alfred Valentine (the current president of Roosevelt Raceway) were subpoenaed. It turned out that the loan was made so Buffalo Racetrack would have enough money in their purse account to open and conduct its meet. After the meet at Buffalo opened, the loan was paid back to Roosevelt Raceway in full within two weeks. This was just the beginning of false allocations made by politicians that Levy would have to fight and prove his innocence throughout his reign at Roosevelt Raceway.

80C3

In 1945, the racing season was more successful than the year before. Roosevelt Raceway was offering purses between $1,000 and $2,000—the highest purses in the entire country.

On August 11, 1945, George Morton Levy would face the first of many scandals which would focus on Roosevelt Raceway. During that time, it was said that "ringers" were being raced at the track (A "ringer" is when a horse is put in a race posing as another horse, who is faster and more competitive, thus deceiving the public). Once again, Levy proved his innocence and Roosevelt Raceway closed that year on a very successful and lucrative note.

How It Began
Opening Night, 1940

The excitement of the opening of Roosevelt Raceway had the employees and establishment working around the clock. Thousands of county residents were employed due to the development of Roosevelt. Many of these workers would have quit their jobs and possibly leave the community for better-paying ones if Roosevelt had not provided the extra employment opportunities. Roosevelt Raceway was definitely an economic and financial asset to the area and the families who lived there. But there was much work that needed to be done and little time to do it. They had to install betting machines, refurbish the racetrack, and print the racing programs. Amazingly, within two months of opening night, they had formed a racing commission, leased the track, and built a paddock area which would accommodate the racehorses. But the toughest task of all was in getting enough horses to fill the racing card for opening night— let alone a twenty-seven-day meet. Perhaps the creating of Roosevelt Raceway was Levy's greatest triumph—for the grandstand, the racetrack, and mutuels were already in place, making it a turnkey operation.

ℴ❦

In life there are certain things that are simply out of a person's control. The first is paying taxes, the second is dying, and the third is the ability to change the weather. Unfortunately, Mother Nature wasn't cooperating with the grand opening of Roosevelt, for three rain cancellations took place: on August 26, 28, and 29. But miraculously, by the end of the week, the weather cleared and 140 horses filled the stable area. They were now ready to rock and roll. On September 2, 1940, with the good Lord smiling down, thumbs up, and all systems go, the doors of Roosevelt Raceway officially opened.

ℴ❦

The time had come! It was opening night and the energy in the air was electrifying and contagious. The flags were blowing in the warm breeze, a band was playing, and the lights shone brightly. The handsome athletic animals proudly paraded in front of the grandstand. Every spectator was busy studying the horses as they trotted by, deciding which pony they would place their bets on. Yes, opening night was definitely exciting and promising to all involved. As it turned out, it was mildly successful, where paid attendance was 4,584 and the betting handle was $40,742. Levy and his associates had expected 15,000 patrons and were somewhat disappointed with the much smaller attendance.

ഉറൗ

Back in the paddock area where the horses nervously waited for their race to be called, the intense energy was overwhelming. The trainers were busy checking and double checking the equipment on their horses before sending them on the track. As the drivers were preparing to jump on their race bikes, the adrenalin of the horses was pumping like that of a triathlon runner waiting for the starting whistle to blow.

ഉറൗ

During that initial meet, drivers such as the legendary Jimmy Jordan, Eddie Cobb, Harry Pownall, Henry Thomas, and Delvin Miller made their racing debuts. It was very exciting to the patrons, for in those days people could freely walk into the paddock to observe the horses and talk to the drivers. This was especially exhilarating to the bettors for it gave a much more personal touch.

The Hot Spot in Town

With all the talk about the new Roosevelt Raceway, it soon became known as the "Hot Spot" in town. Roosevelt was the place where men would dine with their wives or girlfriends, hang out with the guys, and place a few wagers hoping to cash in. During that time there were no casinos, off-track betting parlors, or lottery. The race track was the place to go where a person could gamble in hopes of making some extra money and having some fun. The invigorating new Roosevelt Raceway was the *only* place to go.

After the depression had ended, it led to a greater legalization of gambling. The antigambling mood changed as tremendous financial distress gripped the country, especially after the stock market crash of 1929. People were looking for a place to go to try to recoup some of the financial loses they incurred because of the depression. During that thirty-day meet, the raceway acquired a total attendance of 75,175 and total betting through the mutual machines amounted to $1,200,086. It was a very successful and lucrative venture indeed.

The First Mishap

Roosevelt Raceway was a sight for sore eyes. The beauty it possessed was like no other racetrack in the nation. The glaring lights on the track and the loudspeakers could be seen and heard from miles around. Men and women anxiously looked forward to live racing nights and would count the minutes until post time.

This was also an era of class and sophistication where men attended in suits and fedoras and women would proudly show off their fancy new dresses. Attending Roosevelt Raceway was considered "a night out on the town," where people would strut around in their best attire as if they were royalty.

But in life, nothing is perfect! Whenever there are two objects racing against one another at high speeds, it can be extremely dangerous and there's always the chance of an accident. This holds true for anything: mechanical (cars) or living (people or animals.) Sadly, on June 9, 1941, during a race at Roosevelt Raceway a six-horse pileup occurred. Unfortunately, one horse lost its eye and four drivers were taken to the nearby hospital. The horsemen who witnessed it said it was the worst accident that had occurred since the 1927 Matron Stake. In the race, seven drivers went down and were taken to the hospital. The drivers involved were Harry Pownall, Charley Fleming, Delvin Miller, Eddie Cobb, Ray Nohlechlk and Jim Burlingam.

Major Improvements

In 1941, major improvements to Roosevelt Raceway were being created to make it the finest harness track in the nation. A total of $100,000 was spent in alterations and improvements. Thirteen new barns were built (each with twenty-four stalls) making a total of 312 stalls to house the athletic horses. Also added to the list were two jogging tracks—one that was a third of a mile and another, a mile long. Although it was costly, the improvements and additions that were made appeared to be worth it.

Debts and Loans

By 1942, Roosevelt owner George Levy was saddled with mounting debt. Due to the unexpected war, the racing ceased. He was down to his last cent and had borrowed to the limit. But that didn't stop the relentless, ambitious businessman, for he took up his weary round again with a hope of interesting new capital. Levy would have to quickly raise $25,000 or forfeit the raceway and his dream. It was reported that he received the loan from one of his clients, "Lucky" Luciano.

Although the loan saved his beloved track, this transfer of funds would prove almost disastrous to Roosevelt Raceway, when Levy later came under the investigation of the Kefauver Committee in the 1950s. When questioned of the loan, Levy produced a letter stating that the loan came from his mother.

ℰℭ

The "war years" had taken its toll. Two years later, in 1944, Roosevelt Raceway was once again in dire straits and management was about to be evicted from the premises for $70,000 back rent. George Morton Levy went back to the drawing board, put on his thinking cap, and figured out a way he could get the money. Again, Roosevelt Raceway was saved.

The Starting Gate

The Starting Gate was first introduced to the world by a man named Steve Phillips who happened to be the starter at a racetrack in North Randell, Ohio. Little did Mr. Phillips or anyone else realize that this funny looking vehicle (which had an attached gate for horses to line up behind) would be a major key in revolutionizing harness racing. But exactly how did this unique invention—which would change harness racing for the better—come to be? Was it by accident, a stroke of luck, or merely coincidental?

The idea of designing a mobile starting gate came to Phillips one day when he was driving in a car, filming a race. He noticed how comfortable and easy the horses had followed. Up until then, it could take an hour or so for a race to begin, for recalls were a common occurrence, which frustrated everyone involved. Sometimes there could be six or seven recalls in one race, which wasted a lot of time and exasperated everyone. Thus, the fruition of having a starting gate in a horse race became a reality.

The Old vs. the New

The original starting gate was built from a 1932 Ford Model A that Phillips had converted. It had been constructed in a friend of Phillips' (Harley Mitchell) machine shop, and cost a whopping total of $700. First, they removed the top of the Model A. Next, a long flatbed was installed over the rear wheel. They then attached a set of wings that were made out of iron pipes, which provided a strong railing to surround Phillips while standing. The finishing touches was the addition of a rope, a battery powered motor, and some bailing wire. Unfortunately at first, the gate was not accepted by the horsemen or the racetracks, so it sat idle in a garage for the next several years.

In 1945, Phillips was employed as the starter at Roosevelt Raceway. For some time, the management at the track had been relentlessly trying to find a solution to correct the problem of the constant start delays. Phillips informed them of his invention and they agreed to experiment with it. Shortly after, they went into production on the revised gate. They built the new gate with $52,000 of their own money—which consumed their whole bankroll. There is no doubt in anybody's mind that the introduction and perfection of the starting gate was a major factor that changed harness racing and made it the multimillion dollar sport it is today. Because of the invention of the spectacular starting gate that revolutionized harness racing, Steve Phillips, the inventor, was the first inductee into "The Hall of Fame."

There was not much publicity about the new improvised starting gate until May 24, 1946, when it made its debut at the number one harness track in the country: Roosevelt Raceway. Since the gate had not been named yet, some people described it as a "mobile starting apparatus." Others called it "the starting machine" or simply "the machine." But everyone agreed that it was "the greatest thing since sliced bread!"

Ready to Rock-n-Roll

With the opening of the track, some people came to be part of the exciting meet, while others simply came to see the introduction of Stephen Phillips' "motorized starting barrier," as it was now being called. On opening night, a total of 14,189 spectators were on hand to see the gate make its spectacular debut. Unlike the previous model, the revised gate was built by a Long Island aircraft company using a Chrysler automobile. It had ten scoring positions on its wings, which allowed an eight-foot space for each horse. The gate also used a hydraulic system to open and close the gate's wings.

To everyone's surprise, the gate was even more successful than anticipated. The races went off close to their posted times and everything ran smooth, until one night with a twelve-horse field. Shortly after the gate opened, a horse bore out and rammed into the outside of a wing. When the driver tried to cut into the lead, the wing came back too fast. The mishap by the gate knocked the driver out of the sulky, and rapped the horse sharply in his neck. But the pros of the new starting gate far outweighed the cons. With the introduction of the restyled gate, harness racing had now solved its biggest problem: the monotonous delays in starting a race. Once they perfected the gate and omitted the false starts, attendance skyrocketed. Ironically, one week after the debut of Roosevelt's starting gate, a gentleman named McDonnell introduced his starting gate in Canada.

⅋ⅎ

At that time, the meet at Roosevelt was split with the Old Country Trotting Association. In the years 1950 and 1951, George Morton Levy acted as president and director of the Nassau Trotting Association. Levy was also General Counsel of the Old Country Trotting Association. In 1954, Mr. Levy was elected chairman of the Executive Committee and the director and general counsel. He was said to have sold stock to the legislature who passed the parimutuel laws.

The 1970 International Trot

The new trainer/drivers clubhouse

The starting gate 1957

Aerial view of the starting gate late 1940's

3

Let the Games Begin

"Money, horse racing, and women are three things
the boys just can't figure out."

—Will Rogers

Life in the Fifties

During the fifties, many events occurred which would make
history. The Korean War began, Republican candidate
Dwight D. Eisenhower was inaugurated as the thirty-
fourth President of the United States, and it was in the
fifties that rock and roll music entered the mainstream with
the record "Rock Around the Clock" by Bill Haley and His
Comets, becoming the first record to top the Billboard
magazine pop charts.

It was also an extremely exciting time when an unknown
man who came from the south would pave the way that
would change rock and roll forever. His name was Elvis
Aaron Presley. Elvis "The Pelvis" would become known as
one of the most significant cultural icons of the twentieth

century. And on the fateful day of September 30, 1955, an unfortunate incident took place that would leave millions of women heartbroken. Actor James (Byron) Dean, the cultural icon of teenage disillusionment, was involved in a fatal car accident, which would take his life. And for all you "Big Mac" lovers, it was in 1954 that Ray Kroc bought the first McDonalds franchise.

₧₧

Back in Westbury, New York, at Roosevelt Raceway, the world of harness racing would be changed forever with the invention and introduction of the revised starting gate. With the impressive success of the starting gate, the top drivers in the country began shipping in and racing at Roosevelt. Another reason for the unanticipated popularity by world-class drivers was that Roosevelt Raceway offered the highest purses in the country. That is why the crème de la crème came to race there.

But the sudden demand at Roosevelt made it extremely difficult for a trainer or driver to get acceptance to be stabled on the grounds, for there was only so much room to house the horses. Because of the lack of space, the management was very selective which trainers and horses would be welcomed to their track. Unfortunately, many horsemen were turned away for the stable area was full and could not accommodate any more horses. At that time, it was quite an honor for horsemen to say they were racing at the famous Roosevelt Raceway.

The Dreamtrack

By 1956, the original Vanderbilt grandstands that became Roosevelt Raceway were burdened by excessive additions and dangerous decay. Within the next season, the spectacular new clubhouse/grandstand/track replaced the original Vanderbilt track without any interruption of the racing schedule. The contemporary building was designed by a well-known architect named Arthur Froelich who had designed many other innovative modern structures. The architectural plans cost $400,000 and the building was proposed at a whopping $12,000,000. In the end, the new "Dream Track" (as it was named) cost a total of $20,000,000. The tote board alone cost a whopping $800,000.

But, to Levy and his associates, it was worth every penny. They were the proud proprietors of the most beautiful racetrack in the country. The layout of the grandstand area was impeccably designed. It was positioned in a semicircle facing east, which caught the southeasterly breeze, making it comfortable for the patrons on a hot and steamy night. Also, the grandstand provided air-conditioning for the patrons.

Amidst the grandstand was a formal garden which was designed by Allen Dalsimer of Long Island. The new plant (which consisted of five levels) had suspended security levels in between and boasted eight escalators leading to two restaurants, a coffee shop and a grill room. Sitting on top of the grandstand, almost a hundred feet above the racing strip, was the posh Cloud Casino, which comfortably seated nine hundred patrons. The state-of-the-art grandstand also possessed a fourteen-bed hospital with a fully functional operating room and two restaurants that were owned by concessioner Harry M. Stevens.

Shortly after the opening, a new synthetic track was constructed which had more than 105,000 watts of lights to light up the homestretch. Another unique quality at

Roosevelt was the closed circuit televising of each race, which was broadcast throughout the grandstand for all to watch.

Triple Crown of Harness Racing

George Morton Levy was always thinking of new ways to create revenue for his track and how to enhance the world of Harness Racing. Levy founded a series of three races which were called "The Triple Crown of Harness Racing." The three comprised races were The Cane Pace, The Little Brown Jug, and the Messenger Stakes.

On June 30, 1956, the track hosted the first inaugural Messenger Stakes, which was part of the new "Triple Crown of Harness Racing for Pacers." The race was named in honor of a horse named Messenger who was foaled in England (1780–1808) and later brought to the United States. Since its inauguration in 1956, only ten horses have ever won the Pacing Triple Crown. They are:

1. Adios Butler (1959)
2. Bret Hanover (1965)
3. Romeo Hanover (1966)
4. Rum Customer (1968)
5. Most Happy Fella (1970)
6. Niatross (1980)
7. Ralph Hanover (1983)
8. Western Dreamer (1997)
9. Blissful Hall (1999)
10. No Pan Intended (2003)

The first Messenger was won by Billy Haughton, driver and trainer of the great filly *Belle Acton*, who tied the track record and won $32,320 in purse money. Her stable mate, a colt named *Bachelor Hanover*, finished second. (Bachelor Hanover was also trained by Billy Haughton.) Unable to drive both horses, Haughton put up his friend Stanley Dancer to drive *Bachelor Hanover.*

To George Morton Levy, the founding of "The Triple Crown of Harness Racing" would be just another added credit and achievement in bettering the sport of harness racing. (For more on Haughton, go to drivers section in back of the book).

The International Trot

In 1959, a trotter from France named Jamin was scheduled to run in the inaugural International Trot which was being held at Roosevelt Raceway. Joe Goldstein, who at the time was the track's publicist, spread the word that Jamin's chances would be affected by the loss of over 150 pounds of artichokes. Goldstein said crates of artichokes had been impounded and then misplaced by the United States Department of Agriculture at Idlewild Airport. The track's unbeatable publicity team, Nick Grande, Joey Goldstein, and Lew Barasch, wasted no time in taking advantage of the situation by issuing press notices. Goldstein immediately placed ads in the *New York Times* and *New York Herald Tribune* that read "French Trotter Needs Artichokes. Can you help?" The AD included the phone number at Roosevelt Raceway as the contact information. Local newspapers gave the story extensive play, stating that locals were bringing their backyard-grown artichokes to the track, and United Airlines was flying artichokes in from Watsonville, California (the artichoke capital of America), specifically for the French horse. A few days later, Goldstein said that the horse was reenergized after devouring the artichokes.

Ironically, Jamin went on to win the race in front of a record breaking crowd of 45,723 spectators. The Italian horse Tornese placed second by a mere half a length, and the American entry(the betting favorite), a horse named Trader Horn, finished third(2-1/2 lengths behind Tornese). The mile-and-a-half race was won in a speedy time of 3:08 3/5. Whether it was the fact that the French horse devoured the artichokes or that he was just the best is anyone's guess. (For more on the international races, go to Book Two).

ℬℛ

On August 20, 1960, attendance at Roosevelt was 54,861 (with a racing card that included the International Trot), which at the time was the largest crowd to witness a horse race in the US. A nine-year-old horse named *Hairos II*, steered by driver Willem Geersen, went on to win the mile-and-a-quarter event in the time of 2:34, defeating the Italian horse *Crevalcore* by a half-length. The American horse *Silver Song*, the 9 to 5 favorite, finished third, a mere half-length behind *Crevalcore*. The crowd eclipsed the previous record of 50,337 which was set at the track in August 1957. For twenty-five years, from 1951 to 1975, Roosevelt Raceway's nightly attendance averaged a whopping fifteen thousand. From 1957 to 1967, attendance topped twenty thousand patrons per night. Even though at that time they didn't race during the winter months, the track still drew number-breaking crowds in the frigid temperatures. No other racetrack in the country could come close to the amount of money that was being bet at Roosevelt.

Roosevelt Racetrack was the place to be seen and to people watch for you never knew who would be there.

The popular racetrack drew people from all walks of life: the wealthy, the blue-collar working man, and the familiar faces of celebrities. People would drive for miles just to dine at the posh Cloud Casino restaurant. In fact, on big nights (like the Roosevelt International), you could hardly find a parking space. During that time, it wasn't uncommon for people to park at the adjoining hotels, restaurants, or even on the side of the Meadowbrook Parkway. If you didn't know someone you were unlikely to even get a spot in valet. To this day, people say they remember driving past the track early in the evening and seeing the place illuminated like Disneyland. Yes indeed, every night at Roosevelt Raceway was "a night to remember."

ഗ൪

Roosevelt's cousin, Yonkers Raceway, which was forty minutes away, was no slouch either. During those days, trainers, drivers, and bettors would alternate meets back and forth, as did the thoroughbred tracks Belmont and Aqueduct. It was a "gamblers paradise" where players would racetrack hop in hoping to cash a "big" one.

Part II

Politicians (L-R) Pfeiffer, Sprague, Dewey and Hanley

Frank Costello

Levy testifying

4

Politicians and the Games They Play

The Moreland Act Commission

The Mooreland Act was an act passed by the New York Legislature that was signed into law in 1907. In the forties and fifties, Governor Thomas Dewey successfully used Moreland Commissions to investigate private citizens who were doing business with the government. Public hearings began taking place by the Moreland Act Commission, who, at the time, was investigating New York's top trotting tracks. It was found that top leaders of the Republican Party and a few Democrats who were no longer active politically were reaping huge profits from the racetracks.

Testimonies at the hearings showed that influential politicians acquired substantial blocks of stock in tracks and racing associations. Stocks were being obtained by the politicians at bargain rates and shares were being secretly held in the names of friends and relatives, which were later sold at fabulous gains. Some of the Republicans involved were State Chairman Dean P. Taylor,; State Senator Arthur H. Wicks; J. Russell Sprague, Nassau County leader; former national committee man Alger B. Chapman (who directed Governor Dewey's campaigns in 1946 and 1950); Secretary of State Thomas J. Curran; and Republican leader of New York County and former Assemblyman, Norman F. Penney. Democrats included former State Senator John J. Dunnigan of Manhattan (co-author of the parimutuel law with Mr. Penney); William Weisman, attorney for the late Irwin Steingut; and former State Senator Thomas I. Sheridan and Arthur Lynch who were former Deputy City Treasurers of New York in the O'Dwyer administration.

There were two other men involved who were union officials (hired as labor consultants by the tracks) who had also obtained stock. They were Frank Costello, who was the "Prime Minister of the Underworld," and the son of Frank Erickson, the notorious gambler and New York's largest bookmaker, who became known among other bookmakers nationwide for handling "lay-off bets."

Politics, Crime, and a Professional Spectator Sport

During that time, there was much turmoil in keeping the bookmakers away from the track. The racetracks were a "bookmakers' utopia." They created an incredible amount of money by wagering off-track bets that were being made on the horses. When the commissioner got word of this, he threatened to shut down the tracks. Immediately, Roosevelt Raceway owner George Morton Levy sought refuge and hired the biggest bookmaker, a man named Frank Costello, to help keep bookmakers away.

ﮭﮭﮭ

In 1945, when Russell Sprague (the Chief Executive of Nassau County, a monetary advisor, and owner of Cedar Point Trotting Association) moved into Roosevelt as a tenant, the Republican leader invested $2,000 for his 40 percent of Cedar Point's shares. Ten months later, Mr. Sprague sold his shares for $195,000 because "he did not want his track connections to interfere with his duties as Nassau County executive." (The county had tried unsuccessfully to cut in for 2 percent of the betting revenue.) In 1947, after the CPTA went belly up, Sprague secured $1,000 worth of shares in its successor (the Nassau Trotting Association) which he would sell in 1953 for $64,000. Three years later, in 1950, Sprague purchased $80,000 of stock in the new Yonkers TA, which paid him $88,000 in dividends. As a result of its investigation and hearings, the Moreland Commission recommended a larger share of betting revenue for the state, stricter union controls at the tracks, open ownership of stock, and the elimination of joint control of the tracks and other reforms.

ﮭﮭﮭ

Soon thereafter, Governor Dewey asked for legislation to carry out the recommendations of the commission. At the hearing, the commission placed the evidence on the record but did not spell out its political import. What emerged nonetheless was proof that politicians had made large and small fortunes out of harness racing. Whether any political favors were performed in return for the financial favors was not divulged. But one thing was clear: the ordinary, blue-collar working citizen was not invited to strike it rich.

Joe Adonnis

Frank Erickson

Lucky Luciano

5

Hearings, Testimonies, and Proceedings

"A dog may be man's best friend, but
the horse wrote history."

—Unknown

In the year 1953, investigations were being issued by the Senate Crime Investigating Committee. But it wasn't until the next year that the actual hearings occurred. The first witness to be called was George Morton Levy, who described himself as "a lawyer and President of the Nassau County Trotting Association Inc." On the stand, Mr. Levy testified that, in 1946, the late Benjamin Downing (then chairman of the New York State Harness Racing Commission) threatened to revoke the track's license unless the bookmaking that was being done there ceased. The lawyer stated that Frank Costello was the one man who could keep the track free of bookmakers. The only problem was that Commissioner Downing was unfamiliar with Costello's reputation. When asked if Levy knew Costello, he admitted he had played golf with him several times but they never discussed Costello's affairs. Levy said he had never handled his business affairs and didn't know what his income was, it's source, or if it was legitimate or not. He went on to say that the only time they had ever done business together was fifteen years earlier when Costello had an income tax matter in Washington and Levy flew there to see a representative of some bureau. George Morton Levy said that he went to Costello and told him he would like to hire him to keep gamblers away from the track. Costello told Levy he would do what he could. Levy insisted that Costello be monetarily reimbursed for his services. Although Costello said there was no need, the bookmaker would eventually get compensated for his work. Levy later admitted that he paid Costello a total of $60,000 ($15,000 a year for four years) for his services.

Frank Erickson

Next, the court asked Levy what his relationship was with professional gambler and bookmaker Frank Erickson. Levy admitted he had known Erickson for twenty years and that he had played golf with him, along with Costello and Joseph Schoenbaum (At the time, Joseph Schoenbaum was an employee of the Bureau of Internal Revenue). Levy said that Mr. Schoenbaum had made a large sum of money from stock he owned in the race track and, in 1947, he hired James Watson (son-in-law of Erickson) to go to Detroit and report to him on the availability of a race track site there. He went on to say that at a later date, he employed Watson (at $7,500 a year) to look into whether or not there were other racing interests who intended to purchase Yonkers Raceway, and whether Erickson was interested in the deal.

Frank Erickson was then called to testify, accompanied by his attorney, Harold H. Corbin. Corbin spoke for his client. He informed them that Erickson was presently serving a jail sentence in connection with bookmaking charges in the state of New York, along with charges in the state of New Jersey and income tax fraud charges. Erickson's attorney also stated that his client was being charged with associating with nationwide racketeering syndicates.

Joe Adonnis: A Shady Restaurateur

Next called to testify was a man named Joe Adonnis. He owned and operated a popular Brooklyn restaurant where politicians would often gather. He also operated many gambling houses throughout the state of Florida. Once on stand and under oath, Mr. Adonnis refused to testify against himself in any respect. He also refused to answer a question as to whether he had ever made a "political contribution" to any city, state, or national campaign. He stated the reasons why he felt it necessary to avail himself of his constitutional privileges was because members of the committee and members of the federal government had been publicly proclaiming that he was a member of a nationally organized crime syndicate, and were trying to link him directly to organized crime. Adonnis went on to say that the press alleged that he was a member of a crime syndicate in Chicago and also a member of an organization known as the "mafia," which controls crime on an interstate and national basis.

Jimmy Hoffa

James Cagney presenting trophy for the 1944 Hambletonian

6

Scandals and Struggles for Control

"There's nothing so good for the inside of a man as the outside of the horse."

—Ronald Reagan

By the time the fifties rolled in, harness racing was the fastest growing spectator sport in the United States. It drew larger crowds than any other sport in the nation. The crowds soared thirty-four times what they were since the track opened in the forties. For the owners of Roosevelt Raceway, it was too good to be true, and as the saying goes, "When something looks too good to be true, it usually is."

Taking a Piece of the Pie

In the eleven states that gambling was legal, an astounding $362,668,886 was poured into parimutuel machines from bets made on the trotters and pacers. But the machines paid back only $305,000,000, which was to be divided between the winning tickets. Something didn't quite add up. The math wasn't right. Where did the remaining $57,000,000 go? Nearly all of it was split among the state governments and thirty race tracks from Maine to California. The "bite," as it was called ($37,000,000), went to the race track operators. Of the remaining $20,000,000, New York State received $14,360,040; Illinois took $1,672,603; Maryland got $997,295; California $988,178; Michigan $776,612; Massachusetts $590,308; New Jersey $235,919; Maine $224,750; Ohio $211,472; Delaware $100,331; and Kentucky received $73,914.

What had evolved into a billion-dollar industry attracted a flock of greedy birds anxiously waiting to take their share of crumbs which were thrown to them. The species of these birds were not pleasant hummingbirds or beautiful peacocks. They were extortionists, politicians, dishonest labor leaders, crooked gamblers, and underworld tycoons, all seeking a legalized field where to invest their loot from illegal ventures.

During that time, attendance at parimutuel tracks had skyrocketed, totaling 7,913,344 persons (of whom 4,361,202 were at the New York tracks). The state of New York was the biggest and had the most money bet in harness racing in the union and was the most racket-ridden. There were eight harness horse tracks in New York alone.

In first place, by popular demand, was Roosevelt Raceway—the track that introduced most of the innovations that had built harness racing into the major American sport it is today. Roosevelt was the first track to make changes that would set the pace to where the sport of harness racing would eventually go. It was also among the first tracks to abolish the multiheat system and to offer a straight card of eight races, each with different horses. Roosevelt also stepped up the liveliness of "a night at the races" and the opportunities for wagering by reducing "dead time" through the installation of the mobile starting gate.

Scandals

"A Hambletonian horse gets a little help from his friends."

One year, a riot occurred when it was rumored that a horse in the prestigious race, the Hambletonian, had been drugged. It was said that a horse who had participated in the race at Goshen, New York, and later at Roosevelt Raceway had been "hyped up." People were outraged that a helpless animal had been given illegal drugs for the sake of cashing a ticket. Immediately, animal activists were alerted and called to investigate. At first, the use of the needle went undetected by local racing officials. It came to light only when an owner/driver confessed at a hearing called by the Michigan State Harness Racing Commission, before whom he had been called about another asserted misdeed. That incident would be the induction of enforcing strict laws forbidding the illegal use of drugs in horses in order to enhance their performance. Today, these laws are still stringently enforced in all states.

Jimmy R. Hoffa

Reports from the correspondents of the *New York Times* in various states showed that James R. Hoffa, a labor boss with a police record, owned stock in race tracks in the Midwest where he was also trying to seize control of the track workers. Hoffa, vice president of "The International Brotherhood of Teamsters, AFL," was convicted on conspiracy charges in trying to force independent grocers into a union but escaped with a suspended sentence. His record also showed arrests on assault and extortion charges. At the time, Hoffa owned six thousand shares in the Columbus Trotting Association at Hilliard, Ohio. His chief assistant in the teamsters union was a man named Owen B. Brennan, who also owned six thousand shares of the Hilliard Raceway. At that time, Brennan was racing his own stable of trotters in the Midwest, while he was acting as district commissioner of the United States Trotting Association. The two men were attempting to complete their circle of operations by seizing control of harness track labor in Michigan from the Building Service Employees Detroit local, which was later suspended. It is not known what the outcome of Hoffa's ventures and harness racing business was, for although his disappearance had become known to all, it is said that he was garroted by Anthony "Tony Pro" Provenzano, a notorious New York mobster in Inkster, Michigan, and fed into a wood chipper.

Part III

George Morton Levy, Bob Johnson, and Alvin Weil

Ground breaking ceremony 1956

Ground breaking ceremony 1956

7

It Only Gets Better

"A horse is an angel without wings."

George Morton Levy was at it again! There was no stopping this genius. He was the central figure at the ceremonies to break the ground for a new $20,000,000 harness racing plant at Westbury, Long Island. At the groundbreaking were eleven bronze- and silver-plated shovels, which were being held by executives of Roosevelt Raceway. Nassau County officials and others connected to the sport dug into the hard dirt that had originally formed part of the polo layout of the old Meadowbrook Club. The digging of the shovels was a signal that started a dozen huge earth-moving machines grading the land, uprooting trees and finally demolishing a twenty-year old concrete and steel polo grandstand.

Fifteen years earlier, George Levy had gone out on a limb. He mortgaged his home, pawned the family jewels, and ignored the remarks said by skeptics to launch harness racing on the site that originally had been set up as an automobile racing track. Levy had seen Roosevelt Raceway rise from a few dilapidated sulkies and spavined trotters and pacers into an institution that returned $12,226,807 to the state of New York that year. During the construction of the new plant, there would be no interference with harness racing since the races would be raced on the current land. The new grandstand (made of steel and concrete) would be 800 feet long with a depth of 200 feet and would accommodate 13,750 patrons. Assisting Levy in the groundbreaking exercises were Martin W. Littleton (a former Nassau County attorney with whom Levy was associated), J. Alfred Valentine (the executive vice-president and general manager of the track), Robert G. Johnson (the track president), George P. Monoghan (the New York State Harness Racing Commissioner), Harry Starr and George Gregory (the track vice-presidents), Alvin Weil (the track secretary), A. Holly Patterson (the county executive of Nassau), Francis P. Smith (the president of the Standardbred Owners Association), and State Senator William S. Hults, Jr.

The breaking of the ground was big news, attracting a lot of media and publicity. Attending the exercises that day were a thousand enthusiastic people, who later were the special guests of the Raceway at a buffet luncheon held on the clubhouse terrace. Under the measure adopted by the legislature, the state agreed to yield to the harness tracks half of all the parimutuel revenue above $25,470,000 a year. Hults had sponsored the bill that provided for return of revenues to the track for improvements. The money retained by the tracks were said to be used for construction projects.

A Marriage Made In Heaven

They say that being in partnership is like being married, and in the case of Levy and Weil, it appeared to be a marriage made in heaven. In his early years, Alvin Weil had been a factory worker who turned out cheap celluloid toilet articles in order to pay his tuition through Brooklyn Law School. He toiled at the celluloid bench during the day and attended law classes at night. In 1931, Weil's endless nights of studying paid off. As soon as he passed the bar exams, he began seeking a job more suited to his talents. Weil set his sights on a popular law firm in Freeport that seemed busier than others. The firm was occupied by a man named George Levy, whose reputation as being "the fair and square attorney" had brought him more cases than he could handle himself. After Weil patiently waited hours to see Mr. Levy, his persistence paid off. Weil was hired on the spot after Levy admired the young man's patience, clean appearance, determination, and "sparkle in his eyes." The union would prove to be a long-lasting, pleasant, and profitable one for both men.

The Big Five

Shortly after the breaking of the ground, Levy headed a group that bought the land and set up the new highly successful racetrack. Along with Levy in the venture were J. Alfred Valentine (a Long Island real estate expert), Robert Johnson (a stock broker), Harry G. Starr (a mercantile executive), and Alvin Weil (secretary). These five men, who were neighbors and friends, would become known as "The Big Five," for together, they took a big gamble. Fortunately, the risk paid off. In 1953, "The Big Five" collaborated and laid out plans for expansion to the racetrack. Young Weil, who acted as the group's secretary, was saddled with most of the planning. But in the end, the rolling of the dice paid off for the five men, in a big way. In 1955, business at Roosevelt was roughly one hundred times better than it had been in 1941. During that time, the top night at Roosevelt drew 35,000 customers and 9,136 cars were parked on the premises. For Weil, this was a far cry from the $0.30 celluloid gadget days!

Billy Haughton winning the 1967 Dexter Cup
with Flamboyant

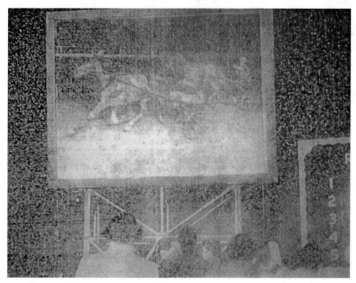

Finiscope

Campaign Ads

8

Advertising Campaigns and the Introduction of Finiscope

"When a jockey retires, he just becomes
another little man."

—Eddie Arcaro

Once the new grandstand was in place, the management launched an extensive campaign aimed at making Roosevelt Raceway an attraction. It began by placing advertisements in all the New York City papers, and also three in Long Island papers. There were full-page ads placed in the publications, along with television, radio, and three major magazines: *The New Yorker*, *Cue*, and *Sports Illustrated*. The theme was to promote the track "as a show place and amusement center," said M. J. Kleinfeld.

Mr. Kleinfeld was the chairman of Heineman, Kleinfeld, Shaw and Joseph, Inc. (formerly the Franklin Bruck Advertising Corporation, which was Roosevelt's agency).

Kleinfeld said there would be no attempt to sell trotting itself, as in previous ads of the earlier Roosevelt Raceway. They had been relentlessly working on the new campaign for months, but when asked how much the campaign cost, Kleinfeld refused to divulge the amount, only saying it represented "a substantial appropriation."

Another aspect of the campaign provided for ads on sports pages through the end of the season. It involved three-column advertisements on amusement pages which showed crowded scenes with headings saying "Nothing like it ever happened to you before!" and "Do Something Different Tonight. Come to Roosevelt Raceway." Advertisements were also placed in taxicabs, on Long Island buses, and in railroad stations. Everywhere you looked there was an AD promoting the new Roosevelt Raceway.

Roosevelt Raceway Introduces Finiscope

It was April 29, 1955, when Roosevelt Raceway first introduced the finiscope. Finiscope was a closed-circuit television system that displayed the races projected on a twenty-foot square screen. This incredible invention was developed by television producer Irving Gray, exclusively for Roosevelt Raceway.

The debut of the finiscope was displayed in front of 19,458 excited spectators who were standing in the pouring rain. But the rain didn't stop their parade for the debut of finiscope was a huge success. The twenty-foot screen had been strategically placed at the head of the stretch next to the tote board so everyone could see the race clearly. The spectators who were interviewed afterward raved about the quality of the picture and of the precise view of the finish line. The very first race ever to be shown on finiscope was won by driver Billy Haughton with a horse called LBT Hanover. With the introduction of the finiscope, Roosevelt proved to be far ahead of the times.

Large crowd at Roosevelt

Billy Haughton winning the American Trotting
Championship with Meadow Bright

9

A Perfect Night for a Star to Shine

"There's no such thing as good money or bad money—there's just money."

—Lucky Luciano

George Levy couldn't have asked for a more perfect night. The weather was pleasant and the luminous stars lit up the brilliant sky. But the biggest star that night would prove to be a forty-year-old man named Billy Haughton, who would shine the brightest. Winning races was nothing new for the driver who came from Old Brookville, Long Island, for, by this time, Haughton already had accumulated 2,014 wins under his belt. That was an incredible figure that no other active harness driver could match. But this particular night would be a night everyone would remember. By the end of the night, Billy would go undefeated, guiding home five winners in five races, while only two of the winners were betting favorites.

There were many happy fans that jumped on the Haughton bandwagon that evening, cashing in their winning tickets. One of the winning horses, a two-year-old Good Time colt, started the streak by winning the race in 2:05 3/5 and paid $6.50. Next to follow were winning horses Spring Ginger, a four-year-old trotting mare, who paid $7.60; and Fool's Dandy, a five-year-old gelding. When Haughton rallied his fourth mount, a horse named Smart Money, and took the featured one-mile pace in 2:01.2/5 the winning ticket paid a whopping $31.40.

After winning with Smart Money (and for those people who bet on the horse, it *was* smart money), the judges called Haughton to the paddock telephone to congratulate him. He told the judges, "Before the night started, I thought the only horse with which I had a chance to win was the horse The Twist, who was in the ninth race." The humble horseman said, "All I can say about the first four winning horses is that I couldn't seem to do anything wrong out there."

His fifth drive, a colt named The Twist, went on to perfect Haughton's night, winning an incredible five out of five races, and paid $4.30. Billy was a huge fan favorite who would go on to be one of the best drivers in harness racing history. And the Haughton name would be one of the most popular and respected names in the business. (For more on Haughton, go to the back of the book on the "drivers' section".)

Part IV

10

The Famous Superfecta

Courtroom drawing of Superfecta trial

"It is the public scandal that offends; to sin in
secret is no sin at all."

—Unknown

One, if not *the* biggest scandal in the history of harness
racing, was the legendary superfecta (race fixing) trial that

took place in 1974. The eleven-week trial started on March 18, 1974. It involved eighty-nine witnesses and over ten thousand pages of transcript. The harness drivers named were only arrested and indicted for political exposure in what many called a "tax case involving a group of gamblers who figured out a way of beating the superfecta race." Observers considered it a "tax case against gamblers." And the people who were associated with the case called it "a manufactured case designed by the prosecution to generate the maximum publicity."

‪‭

In the beginning of the trial, the government refused to let the drivers' defense attorneys know what their clients were actually being charged with. Before and during the trial, the government would change their Bill of Particulars five different times. It was said that the drivers were being bribed to make sure they didn't win the race they were in and when that theory didn't hold up, they accused the drivers of being bribed to win their race. Now, if you know anything about harness racing, there is *no* way to bribe a driver to win!

Before the trial started, the defense attorneys went in front of Magistrate Judge Catoggio, demanding that they receive the particulars of the case so they could prepare for the trial. The defense attorneys also were accusing the prosecution of vagueness.

Judge Catoggio said to the prosecution, "Here you have an indictment that was opened on the twentieth of December and had a press interview on television before these men even were arraigned."

The judge continued "All this horn blowing publicity. I think it would be advisable if the prosecution could put on the table what this is all about.... These men are entitled to know exactly when and where you said they committed a crime.... What the subject matter of the alleged bribery was, the sum of money, race tickets, and how it passed hands.... In plain English...when did it happen?" The aggravated judge said, "Give the approximate times, dates, and places of the alleged bribery of each defendant and name the driver and the bribery in each specified race."

The three prosecutors, Dennis Dillon, Hal Myerson and Michael Pollack, could have easily been named Moe, Larry, and Curly for it is how you would expect the Three Stooges to act if they were trying a case.

හ්රා

The accusations started in the summer of 1973. During this time, many of the nation's top harness drivers were all being questioned and interviewed by the FBI. On September 5, 1973, the District Attorney of Nassau County (a man named William Cahn) sent out seven hundred request subpoenas to every driver, trainer, and owner at Roosevelt Raceway. This caused a pandemonium for the requested return date was set a mere two weeks away (September 20, 1973).

Jesse Moss, the SOA attorney, told the members that they did not have to answer the request subpoenas. On September 20, over five hundred of the subpoenaed drivers, owners, and trainers showed up at the court house, filling up three courtrooms. Mr. Cahn, closely followed by the press, went into each courtroom and made the exact same speech. The district attorney told them that his office had been receiving anonymous calls from horse owners reporting race fixing. Cahn said if anyone knew anything about this to please come forward and report it to him.

You could hear a pin drop in the courtroom as everyone went silent in disbelief. Harry Horowitz, a local horse owner, was disgusted and irate. He stood up and said that he had been subpoenaed to show up in court, and was being questioned by family and friends asking what was going on. Horowitz said this was an unjust persecution of innocent men.

ഇരെ

On September 6, 1973, the headlines in the papers read **"Most Superfecta Races at Roosevelt and Yonkers Raceways are fixed! Betting ring netting $2 million."** A week later, on September 14, 1973, some of the top harness drivers in the country were subpoenaed to appear before a grand jury. Those called to appear were Herve Filion, Norman Dauplaise, Buddy Gilmour, Carmine Abbatiello, Lucien Fontaine, Frank Popfinger, Real Cormier, Billy Myer, Maurice Pusey, Gene Mattucci, Benny Webster, Ken McNutt, Mike Santa Maria, Joe Faraldo, Eldon Turcotte, John Barchi, George Foldi, John Miritello, Gerry Procino, Jim Tallman, and Steve Demas. Of the drivers that would later be indicted, there were several names missing. Those names were Del Insko, Billy Hudson, and Dale Ross.

ഇരെ

What caused this unfortunate situation and who were the perpetrators? It started with a woman named Constance Rogers, who was the girlfriend of Forrest Gerry, Jr., known as a high roller who loved betting the horses. Constance was a striking, statuesque woman who demanded attention wherever she went. This stunning lady began cashing multiple superfecta tickets at the OTB (off-track betting) parlor on a regular basis. Miss Rogers would strut up to the betting window and cash as many as five superfecta tickets at the same time. The looker became a regular, raising the eyes of the OTB employees as to how one person could be that lucky in winning so many big races. The employees also noticed that Ms. Rogers was not always alone. There were others with her who were also cashing in multiple superfecta tickets. Feeling that something was not right, the officials at the OTB immediately contacted the FBI with their suspicions. That was the straw that broke the camel's back and started the investigation.

୫୦ଓ

Miss Rogers would later be indicted and convicted (not on race fixing charges but, instead, on three counts of giving false identification to the IRS) when she cashed $57,347 worth of superfecta tickets on three separate occasions: March 21, 1973, April 2, 1973, and April 4, 1973, at OTB parlors. On December 20, 1973, thirteen harness drivers were arrested, indicted, and suspended from driving for supposedly sports bribery charges on conspiring with a betting ring that was said to have netted $2 million on fifty allegedly fixed superfecta races at Roosevelt and Yonkers Raceways (between January 24, 1972, and April 13, 1973).

The drivers named were Del Insko, William "Buddy" Gilmour, Carmine Abbatiello, Real Cormier, Billy Myer, Kenneth McNutt, Eldon Turcotte, Dale Ross, Frank Popfinger, Maurice Pusey, George Foldi, Billy Hudson, and Benny Webster.

୫୦ଓ

On the morning of December 20 (at 5:00 a.m.), NY state and local police as well as FBI agents raided the homes of the drivers in question and took them into custody. At that time, several of the drivers were not at home, but would later turn themselves into the authorities. Driver Billy Myer, known as an early bird, who was at his barn before the break of day, received a call from his girlfriend. The woman told him to come home so he could be arrested. A startled and confused Myer replied, "What?" Shortly after he hung up, Myer returned home where he was met at the door by police and taken away in handcuffs.

හ)(ය

The trial began with the defense attorney posing the question of whether these particular races were the result of race fixing or just extremely good handicapping. Eleven stressful, drawn-out weeks of testimonies were heard from eighty-nine witnesses. Every single witness said "they never saw a driver take a bribe." The only thing that was ever heard was hearsay evidence by Forrest Gerry, Jr. It was said that Gerry told his backers and associates he had bribed drivers, but there was not one shred of evidence proving bribery to any single driver. Mr. Gerry, Jr. simply said that he beat the superfecta by ingenious handicapping.

හ)(ය

By week three of the trial, the government's case started to unravel. Defense Attorney Herb Sterenfeld, who represented Buddy Gilmour, Kenny McNutt, and Benny Webster, asked witness Agent Nicholas Gianturo of the FBI, "Are you telling me that Mr. Gilmour is being charged with bribery in the five races that he won?"

The witness answered, "That is my understanding."

"I see," said Atty. Sterenfeld.

Sterenfeld then asked Gianturo, "What were the odds on Mr. McNutt's horse, Top Tune N?"

"He was 62 to 1," replied Gianturo.

"And are you also telling me that Mr. McNutt was the longest shot in the race who started from post position number eight and he is being indicted for bribery in this race?" said Sterenfeld.

"Yes," the witness replied.

Laughter was heard throughout the courtroom. Soon thereafter, several other things started to emerge, such as the accused betting ring had been omitting the longest shots in a race, and, at other times, they were keying the favorite. These two ways of betting is the *proper* way and how a good handicapper bets.

ഇൽ

The government case centered on those horses that the betting group usually omitted, who were the longest shots in the race. For example, the bettors in question left out the two horses with the longest odds in the race on February 13, 1973, and for an investment of $17,223 made a profit of $105,177. But, of course, they didn't win every race. Nobody can win every time. On other occasions they would lose. Like the time on February 6, 1973, when they left out a horse Del Insko was driving who finished second. One of the backers, a man named David Kraft, stated that he dropped out of the betting group after he had lost nine of the alleged nineteen "fixed" races which he helped the ring to finance.

ഇൽ

The government's alleged "star" witness was a man named Joseph Pullman. At one time, Pullman had been the chauffeur and betting aide for Forrest Gerry, Jr., the accused mastermind of the ring the government says netted $1 million on allegedly fixed superfecta races at Yonkers and Roosevelt. Pullman (known by many as Bear) was a large man with broad shoulders and a cunning smile. When Pullman was called to testify, he reputed his grand jury testimony that he made the previous year stating that the agents and the FBI coached him on what to tell the grand jury. He stated the government had threatened him and told him that if he didn't comply with what they instructed him to say, they would put him in jail.

ℰℭ

Forrest Gerry, Jr. figured out that the average payoff in a superfecta was $3,000. He also discovered that for an investment of $1,060, he could box six horses in a race. At the time Gerry didn't have the funds so he contacted investors to back him, telling them that "they were betting for the drivers" he had bribed to finish out of the top four with their horse in the race. As a professional handicapper and former harness driver himself, he began eliminating the longest shots in the race, and at other times he would "key" a horse to win a race. With this way of handicapping, he began hitting superfectas that were paying big numbers. The defense attorney told the jury that the investment group put up a total of $1,500,000 and netted only $1 million, thus they lost $500,000. Was that such a good investment?

ℰℭ

Next, the prosecuting attorney said that the "ring" had won way too many times—that was the reason why they were being accused of fixing races. The following day the head of the Brooklyn Organized Crime Strike Force, a man named

Denis Dillon, was called to testify. Once on the stand, Dillon said that Pullman confided in him that the previous year Gerry boasted of tying up the Superfecta and having certain drivers in his pocket. He also said Gerry had given different sets of "dead" horses to different sets of bettors.

₧₧

Several more witnesses were called. The witnesses also stated that the government told them what they were to say, and if they didn't do as they were told, they threatened to deport them or send family members to jail. Pullman said that on several occasions, he went to talk to the prosecution and had recorded all conversations on tape. He also told them that one particular prosecutor bragged to him of having the judge in his pocket. The judge immediately disallowed the defense to submit the tapes.

As Pullman got down from the witness stand, another witness came forward who was for the prosecution. The man stated that in the early 1960s he used to give bribes to drivers Buddy Gilmour, Benny Webster, and Kenny McNutt over the fence at Buffalo Raceway. Under cross examination, the defense attorney produced a picture of the fence at Buffalo and asked the witness if this was the fence he was talking about and if the year 1960 was correct. The witness answered 'yes' to both questions.

The defense attorney, a man named Herb Sterenfeld, took out a photo and showed it to the jury which displayed there had been no fence at that track during that time. Sterenfeld went on to say that Gilmour, Webster, and McNutt were not even racing at Buffalo Racetrack during the years in question.

Attorney Sterenfeld (who represented drivers Webster, Gilmour, and McNutt) told the jury, "If a race is fixed you don't bet on the favorites, you bet on Plug and Firehorse?" (Plug and Firehorse are names for broken-down horses). "And if a race is fixed you do not bet $18,000 and win back $12,000. You only need to bet $2.00. That's just common sense," Sternfeld said.

"You could not get these drivers to agree on the time of the day, much less who should win the races. After all, there are purses involved."(When the trial was over, Attorney Sterenfeld was instrumental in winning the case for all thirteen drivers.)

Next, the defense attorneys called George Morton Levy, leading driver and trainer Delvin Miller and Milt Taylor (Director of Racing at Yonkers) to the stand. Levy stated that he thought the superfecta wagering was unfair to the average bettor because a smart handicapper with sufficient funds had a tremendous advantage over the person buying a $3 Superfecta ticket. He explained that in an average race, there were eight horses and a good handicapper could omit two of them and box every other combination for $1,080. At that time, the average superfecta payoff was $3,000, so a good handicapper only had to hit one superfecta out of three to break even. Levy went on to say, "There was no evidence of corruption with the superfecta races. It was just too easy for a good handicapper who had the money to invest."

Next, trainer/driver Del Miller reviewed several of the race films for which driver Del Insko was indicted. After carefully reviewing the tapes, Miller said that Insko gave a supreme effort in every one of the races. Milt Taylor (Director of Racing at Yonkers) also reviewed each Superfecta race in question three times, and said he didn't see anything wrong with any of them. Next, the prosecution started showing videos of the races and told the jury, "In this race we want you to watch the way driver Carmine Abbatiello on the number 3 horse holds his horse back."

As the video began, it portrayed all the drivers and horses positions at the quarter pole. Immediately, Carmine Abbatiello jumped up out of his seat and yelled, "But I'm not even in that race!" More laughter echoed through the courtroom.

The slanderous accusations continued. The prosecution accused drivers Billy Myer and Kenny McNutt of cashing OTB checks at a bank. He said they had many witnesses verifying this but unfortunately was unable to get Billy Myer on camera actually cashing superfecta tickets. The reason was because Myer was too clever and knew exactly where the cameras were located, so he avoided those areas. Myer and McNutt both swore that they had never stepped foot in that bank and volunteered to take a lie detector test, to which the prosecution objected.

ഇരു

The much publicized case was turning into a three-ring circus. When things looked like they couldn't get any worse for the prosecution, they did. An incident occurred one day while the drivers and their attorneys were having lunch in the court house cafeteria. The prosecution and their witnesses were standing at the entrance pointing to the drivers and whispering. After they left, the defense attorneys called all the drivers into the hallway and informed them to go to the restroom and switch clothes with one another. They also told them to switch seats.

When court resumed and the witnesses were called to testify, they identified some of the wrong people. Sportswriter Tony Sisti, who was covering the story for Newsday, was mistakenly identified by one of the witnesses as seen cashing OTB checks at the bank. When the witness identified Sisti as "that man in the gray suit with long sideburns and a red tie", the courtroom was in an uproar. At that point, defense attorney Arnold Roseman shouted indignantly "That's Tony Sisti, a reporter for Newsday." (It seemed that Mr. Sisti was falsely accused for the mere reason he was wearing a red tie and that earlier in the day driver Billy Hudson wore a red tie.) That particular witness had been coached by the prosecution to accuse the man who was wearing a red tie that morning (driver/trainer Billy Hudson.) After the defense attorneys noticed the prosecution coaching witnesses, they told Hudson to take off the tie and switch coats with another person, which he did.

Sisti later said that he had bet the superfecta only twice in his life and lost each time. He went on to say that not only had he never stepped in the bank in question, but he didn't even know where it was located. But even after it was proved that there was no wrongdoing, the damage had been done.

All the bad publicity of the trial had tarnished the reputations of many innocent men. At the end of the trial, the prosecutors were cited for improper conduct. One of the attorneys for the defense was unjustly issued twenty-five counts of "contempt of courts" for his actions during the trial. Even after all these years have gone by and each and every one of the men were acquitted, when mentioning one of the thirteen drivers who were accused in the Superfecta trial, there are still some people who say, "Oh yeah, I remember him. He was the driver who fixed all those races at Roosevelt." Unfortunately that's our society and there are people who will believe whatever they want to. But one thing for sure is that the scandal of the superfecta races at Roosevelt Raceway gave the track and the drivers a lot of publicity. Maybe it wasn't the right kind, but it still was publicity. And as people say, "As long as you spell my name right, it's all good."

The Aftermath

When the trial had ended and the dust had settled, the attorneys' fees to defend the thirteen drivers was astronomical. The irony is that the total lawyer fees added up to the amount they were accused of netting in the "supposedly" fixed races.

Tragically, one of the driver/trainers, a man named Maurice Pusey, would lose everything he owned, including his house and job. Before the trial, Pusey was working as the second trainer for Herve Filion. Occasionally, Filion would put Pusey up to drive his horses—maybe five to ten times a year. One of his mounts happened to be a horse that was in a Superfecta race. The horse had post position number 8 and went off at 28 to 1 odds.

Pusey's boss, Herve, was one of the main targets in the superfecta trial, so, since he was connected to Herve, he also became a target. Pusey said that several times the prosecution told him that if he would tell them something about Herve they would let him go. Maurice would eventually have to sell his house just to pay his attorney fees. After his acquittal, he moved back to Canada. Shortly after, Pusey moved back to the United States and got a job working for Brook Ledge Horse Transportation. He remained working for Brook Ledge until his death in 2008.

Below is the list of the attorneys who represented the drivers:

- **Herb Sterenfeld** represented Buddy Gilmour, Benny Webster and Ken Mc Nutt.
- **William McDaniels** represented Del Insko.
- **Nick Castellano** represented Eldon Turcotte, Dale Ross, Carmine Abbatiello and Frank Popfinger.
- **Arnold Roseman** represented Real Cormier.
- **William Merritt** represented Bill Hudson.
- **Walter Kenny** represented George Foldi.
- **Daniel Hollman** represented Bill Myer and Maurice Pusey.

In all, the drivers were accused of bribery in forty-three superfecta races with not an ounce of evidence against any of them.

1963 stable fire

Race accident

11

Danger and Fatal Occurrences

"The most tangible of all mysteries—fire."

The day was October 14, 1963. It was a day that everybody would like to forget. Even after fifty years have passed, people still recall the tragedy and devastation that occurred on that dreadful night.

What started out as a quiet but windy night at Roosevelt Raceway ended in tragedy, disaster, and death. Sergeant Arthur Bjorn was doing what he did every morning at 4:30 a.m. The security guard at Roosevelt Raceway was making his normal half-hour scheduled rounds, making sure everything was copasetic in the barn area.

Although there was usually never a problem, every now and then a mischievous horse would pull a Houdini and manage to escape from his stall. When this would happen, Bjorn would most likely find the escapee helping himself to some grain in the tack room, or trying to court a mare by bellowing at her through the stall gate. But the morning of October 14 was not of the ordinary. It was every horseman's nightmare.

Slightly after 4:30 a.m., Bjorn discovered a fire had started and was spreading quickly throughout the stable area. The guard immediately called the fire department. Within ten minutes, six fire trucks arrived, accompanied by a hundred volunteers. It appeared that the fire had started in Barn G. Because of the ten-miles-an-hour wind, the flames quickly leaped across a forty-foot-wide barn separation walk area that led to Barn H. The grooms who lived on the track awoke from the smell of the fumes and heavy smoke. They immediately formed a human wall preventing the horses who had escaped from their stalls to return.

But it's a known fact that, in the case of a fire, a horse will try to remain in their stall, which to them is their home and safety. Throughout the stable area, the neighing of the horses and the kicking in their stalls was deafening and heartbreaking to those who were there. Firemen, grooms, and racetrack employees tried fervently to rescue as many of the frightened racehorses as they could. The fumes were overpowering and the sizzling of the metal glass was so hot it burned the hands of some of the firemen.

They were successful in rescuing some of the horses in Barn H by leading them out the backside of the barn to safety. Several of the frightened horses refused to leave their stalls, while others who were brought to safety tried to return to the blazing barn. And the bright lights and the loud siren blaring from the fire trucks did nothing to calm the horses, it only frightened them more. The heart-wrenching scene was like something out of a movie. The only problem was this wasn't a movie, it was real!

At that time, there were two grooms who worked for trainer Tony Abbatiello. The men, named Tommy Luchento and George Berkner, escaped the fire by smashing the tack window and crawling out. Years later, these men would become trainers and drivers themselves, and Luchento would one day become the President of the SBOANJ.

One of the grooms, a man named Randy Perry (who later became a trainer/driver), was working for trainer Hugh Bell at the time. He recalls leading a horse out of the fire to safety. Once outside the stables, Perry noticed that the horse's mane and tail were on fire, so he extinguished the flames with his bare hands. Perry says that, even today, he has nightmares reliving that night.

Early the next morning, a young girl living in a house located near the racetrack woke to find a horse grazing in her backyard. The young child awoke her parents up, showed them the horse, and asked if she could keep him. Of course they immediately called the authorities. Shortly thereafter, the racehorse was returned to its rightful owner. He was one of the few lucky horses who escaped alive that night.

The loss of horses in that fire was estimated at around $250,000 and the damage to the barns was valued at $75,000 each. Driver/trainer Billy Hudson, unfortunately, got hit the hardest, losing thirteen of his horses. Other stables who lost horses that night was Tony Abbatiello (who lost nine) and trainer Howard Beissinger (who lost five) including his stakes-winning champion, Merrie Adios. Hudson's horses were partly insured, while Beissinger's horses were insured for half of their value. It is not known if Abbatiello's horses were covered or not.

Among the unfortunate victims who never made it out that night was a mare named Lady Cindy, who had pleasured many bettors by winning the last race the night before the fire. After a thorough and intense investigation was performed, the detectives who headed the case ruled it as accidental. It was written in the report that the electrical wiring was in good order and the probable cause of the deadly fire was due to a smoldering cigarette. With the devastation caused by the fire, many horsemen's lives would never be the same. Some would lose their livelihood and be forced to say good-bye to what they considered their life: harness racing. Many men and women who were trainers, owners, drivers, and grooms lost a piece of themselves that night, never to get it back again. The loss of the horses was not just of monetary value. It was much more. The horses were family to those people.

Because of the devastation, heartache, and damage done that night, the track management decided not to rebuild new barns. Instead, they would eventually build a recreational basketball court for the grooms to enjoy.

Below is a list of the beautiful horses whose lives were taken because of the fire:

The Billy Hudson Stable

- Mann Hanover
- Real McCoy
- Victory Flush
- Zip Time
- Scotty Winn
- Mighty Knight
- Tarport Andy
- Frisky Andrew
- Calumet Gene
- Carroll Oregon
- Lady Cindy
- Lochinvar Scott
- Francia Byrd

Tony Abbatiello Stable

- Joey Gene
- Bunnie Betty
- Fay's True
- Swift Hanover
- Twinkle Star
- Bally Wick
- My Treasure
- Towne Hanover
- Wise Byrd

Howard Beissinger Stable

- Merrie Adios
- Merrie Bianch
- Merrie Princess
- Parker Time
- Victor

Racehorse Accidents

As stated earlier, whenever there are two objects that are going at rapid speeds, there's a chance an accident might occur. It happens in other sports such as NASCAR and motorboat racing. Unfortunately, it is no different in horse racing (thoroughbred or standardbred). Throughout the years, harness racing has lost some of their best drivers, either in a race or while exercising a horse.

In 1986, harness driver David Dunckley was involved in a four-horse pileup at Roosevelt Raceway. During the race, a horse that was cutting the mile, (leading) driven by Donny Bonacorsa, grabbed his shoe and fell to the ground which caused a chain reaction. Unable to avoid running into Bonacorsa and the horse, driver Herve Filion crashed into them, and David Dunckley collided into Herve Filion. Although this was a horrific accident, Dunckley was the only driver who was unseated, which occurred when he fell out of the modified sulky backwards and hit his head. Dunckley was conscious when he was placed in the ambulance, but, shortly after went into a coma and, sadly, died a few days later. David Dunckley was only forty-seven years old.

In all the years since its inception, there have been way too many accidents that have occurred in the sport of harness racing. Some were caused by a horse and others by a driver. People don't realize how dangerous it can be driving in a horse race. Within a split second, anything can happen. When a driver is sitting behind a thousand-pound animal, with nothing to protect him, his life is in jeopardy the moment he gets on the sulky.

You might ask yourself, why do these men do it? There are several reasons. They do it for the love of the sport, the love of the animal, or to entertain the public. It's just in their blood. Even after some drivers have been involved in accidents, they hop back on the sulky the minute they are able to do so.

Below is a list of other drivers who unfortunately have lost their lives either driving in a race or race related.

- William Haughton, age 61, Yonkers Raceway, died of complications due to being catapulted in a race.
- Shelley Goudreau, age 34, Hollywood Park, died due to severe injuries incurred in a horserace accident.
- Henri Filion, age 55, died from internal bleeding due to a racehorse accident.

- Ken Heeney, age 52, Foxboro, died due to severe injuries.
- Wayne Smullen, age 41, Freestate Raceway, died due to severe injuries incurred in a horserace accident.

To all the drivers who lost their lives and those drivers who put their lives on the line everyday while racing horses to entertain us, may God bless you and keep you safe.

Ed Sullivan

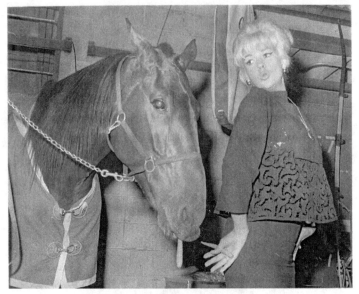

Jane Mansfield and Cardigan Bay

President Lyndon B. Johnson visiting Roosevelt Raceway

12

Celebrities and VIPs

"Champions aren't made in the gyms. Champions
are made from something they have deep inside
them—a desire, a dream, a vision."

—Muhammad Ali

Growing up, George Morton Levy thought he would
become a professional baseball player. He played so well
at Freeport High School (he was a 115- pound shortstop
and football quarterback) that he refused to graduate with
his class in 1905, explaining to his somewhat stunned
parents that he was too young for the rigors of college.
At NYU Law School, Levy master-minded the Great
Baseball Hoax of Rensselaer Tech, becoming one of the
few figures in American sports to happily admit "throwing
a ball game." Levy graduated at the top of his class in law
school, becoming one of the best criminal attorneys the
state of New York would see. His strong suit proved to be
in criminal law.

In the 1930s, the 'Levy' name was something of an eastern seaboard legend. He happily took on the entire state of New York and most of suburban Long Island in a protracted legal engagement known as "that Mineola dog-track ruckus," which he finally won. His popularity and success in winning many 'high-profile' cases brought Levy many colorful new friends. As mentioned ,among his golf partners were two fellow islanders named Frank Costello and Frank Erickson. But, although Levy was a friend to all and remained loyal to each and every one of his friends, in some cases, he admitted, it cost him much. So it is no wonder that when George Morton Levy founded and ran the controversial and exciting Roosevelt Raceway, it would attract people from "all walks of life." Movie stars, sport celebrities, gangsters, and politicians would attend the stimulating Roosevelt Raceway. On any given day, you might catch a glimpse of the President of the United States (Lyndon B. Johnson); Rowan and Martin (*Laugh In*) getting a ride on a jog cart; the Rangers, led by Gilles Villemeure; Charlie Keller (New York Yankees and the founder of Yankeeland Farms); Jack Dempsey (famous boxer); James Cagney (actor); Mickey Mantle (famous ball player); Ed Sullivan ("The Ed Sullivan Show"), George Steinbrenner (owner of New York Yankees, investor, and entrepreneur); Joey Heatherton (actress); Milton Berle (comedian); Mickey Rooney (actor); Bob Hope (comedian and actor); and Debbie Reynolds (actress).

Some other celebrities who made Roosevelt Raceway their choice for fine dining, horse racing,, and gambling were Sugar Ray Robinson, Cab Calloway, George Foreman, Joe Klecko, Jerry Koosman, Ed Kranepool, Ed Westfall, Charo, Billy Hampton, Walt Michaels (the NY Jets), Jay

Black from Jay and the Americans (singer), Dara Torres, Wayne Chrebet, Jimmy Durante and the gorgeous actress Zsa Zsa Gabor. In February 1958, an episode of *The Lucille Ball–Desi Arnez Show* was shot live at Roosevelt Raceway. At that time, *The Lucille Ball* show was the number one show in America. It was an episode about Lucy winning a race horse for her son, Little Ricky. But in order for her to keep the horse, she had to enter the horse in a race at Roosevelt Raceway.

One night at Roosevelt, the lucky patrons who were there got to see a famous, beautiful redhead. Her name was Tina Louise (actress on *Gilligan's Island*) who was appearing at the track to do a publicity stunt. As many elated men watched, Ms. Louise gave a goat to a French horse that was to race in the 1961 International Trot. On the international flight from France to the States, a goat who was the French horse's stall companion was not allowed to fly into the States. Without his small stall mate, Jamin (the French horse) became very depressed and wouldn't eat so the horse's trainer purchased another goat for him, which Ms. Louise presented.

₭₩₲

It has been said that George Morton Levy created what many people say was the "eighth wonder of the world." Roosevelt Raceway attracted people from the corners of the world. During the years Roosevelt Raceway was operating, it was the ultimate recreational venue. But the action and excitement didn't just happen during the evening hours when the track announcer cried, "And the marshal calls the pacers." In the more than forty years Roosevelt Raceway was open, there were many famous people who were personally involved in the sport of harness racing. One of the most prominent and renowned celebrities was a man who not only owned race horses, but owned a major sport team. His name was George Steinbrenner.

It was just a normal day at the Billy Haughton Stable. The grooms were busy tending to their horses: harnessing them, then bathing and cooling them down after they had finished going their training miles. As a car pulled up in front of the Haughton stable, a large and handsome man got out of the car, followed by two men. To the grooms and second trainers at the barn, these three men looked familiar. The trainer of the stable, Billy Haughton, came out of his office and invited the men to come inside. The caretakers of the horses soon discovered that the three men were none other than George Steinbrenner (the owner of the New York Yankees), Whitey Ford (pitcher for the Yankees), and Mickey Mantle (center fielder for the Yankees). This particular day was going to be a special one for these super-stars, for it would be a day of training. It was the first time these three sport figures would sit behind a horse and train. They went there to prepare for an upcoming celebrity race which would be held several weeks away at Pompano Park Racetrack, in Pompano Beach, Florida. Today, these men would step "outside the box" and learn the ways of one of the nation's best sports—harness racing.

Although this was an exciting time for the trio, this was just the beginning for George, for he would fall in love with the sport and be actively involved in it up until the time of his death. During that time, George was good friends with acclaimed drivers Stanley Dancer, Del Miller, and Bill Haughton, so it didn't take long before Steinbrenner was 'hooked' on the sport and the thrill of owning and racing horses. People who knew George said that harness racing was his true passion and his way to relax after a long and nerve-wracking season of baseball. When George sat on the sulky and let the horse guide him around the track, he was in his glory. And as impetuous as he could be with his New York Yankees, George was patient and low key when it came to horse racing.

Steinbrenner was used to cracking the whip now and then with his World Series–winning team, so sitting in a sulky with a whip in his hand came natural. During his career in harness racing Steinbrenner purchased many horses. One was a horse named Incredible Finale, which he had purchased for $300,000. Incredible Finale was named the "1986 Illinois Harness Horse of the Year" and earned $700,000 for his owner. Up until his death in 2010, George owned many harness horses, thoroughbreds, and, at one time, owned Tampa Bay Downs. Harness racing lost a huge fan and fellow horsemen when George passed away at age eighty.

It would be fair to say that Roosevelt Raceway paved the way for future venues like Atlantic City, Las Vegas, and racetracks around the nation, where a person could go to gamble, be entertained (by the races), and watch beautiful and famous people. Roosevelt Raceway was "where it all began."

Billy Myer with Jesse Owens

I Love Lucy official cast photo

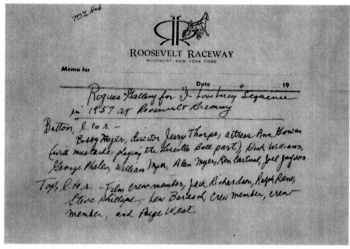

I Love Lucy official cast

Debbie Reynolds and George Morton Levy

Unidentified person, Joey Heatherton and George Morton levy

Part V

Countess Adios winning the 1960 Messenger

13

The Famous Races at Roosevelt

Miss Universe 1976 Rina Messinger
presenting trophy to Bobby Vitrano

The International Trot

The International Trot was a racing event that took place at Roosevelt Raceway in Westbury, New York. Unlike other typical races, the International Trot was created in 1959 by Roosevelt founder George Morton Levy. The purpose of the race was to convince drivers and trainers across the world to bring their best trotter to compete against the top trotters in the United States. (In Canada, a horse was "invited" every year to participate in the prestigious race.)

The International Trot was a series that took place over three weeks. The first race was called the "American Trotting Championship". The horses that finished first and sometimes the second place finisher would go on to represent the United States in the International Trot. Week two of the series was called The International. In The International, the horses representing their country would race against one another, vying to win the title. After the race was over and the winner was named, the top finishers would return the next week to compete in the Challenge Cup against selected horses from the American Trotting Championship.

As you can imagine, the International Series required a lot of planning and lots of special approvals. This included waivers from national and local agencies. Besides the sensational International Trot there were some patrons who came to see the "two-legged fillies." At that time, the Miss Universe Pageant took place in neighboring Atlantic City, New Jersey. While the International Trot was going on, contestants from the pageant would come to Roosevelt to pose alongside the horses and mingle with the enthusiastic crowd.

After Roosevelt Raceway closed its doors in 1988, the International Trot moved to its sister track, Yonkers Raceway. But the excitement of watching the world champion horses compete, the beauty queens parading about, and the wild wagering that the International Trot provided will always remain loyal to its founder: Roosevelt Raceway...where it all began!

❧☙

Another great race that took place at Roosevelt Raceway was The Messenger. Drawing for post positions in that race was almost as exciting as the race itself. In 1967, the drawing took place in Locust Valley, Long Island (about ten miles from Roosevelt Raceway), and a few feet away from the grave of the famous horse, Messenger. The drawing was conducted by Presiding Judge Charlie Plumb. That particular year, the track sent out eight homing pigeons, each carrying a horse's name and post position. It took the pigeons an hour and a half to complete the task. Waiting for the couriers to return to the track were more than fifty excited reporters from newspapers, magazines, television, and radio, along with a journalism class from LIU. The previous year the results were electronically flashed from the top of the Empire State Building in Morse code.

❧☙

The International, like all major sporting events was covered by an overflow of media members. This usually included a large contingent of foreign press. The evening of the big race would start out with a cocktail reception for media members and their spouses. After the reception had ended, everyone was off to the fabulous Cloud Casino for a gourmet dinner. During that time of year, when these famous races were run, the residents of Long Island and horsemen around the world anxiously waited to see what new racing records would be set that year. (For more on the International Race, the winners, and the purses, go to section in the back of the book.)

Quick Song winning 1960 Dexter cup
with press box in the background

Roosevelt Raceway Parties

Levy and his daughter CeCe at a party

14

The Press Box
and the Parties

Picture of a Trot race

Nevele Pride 2nd from left Dexter Cup

PR man Joey Goldstein, his wife Helene
and George Morton Levy

Levy family

"I don't know a lot about politics, but I can
recognize a good party when I see one."

—Mae West

There was much more to the famous International Trot
which was held every August at Roosevelt Raceway than
just watching the top trotters in the country compete.
Months before the race took place, invitations were sent
out for the top trotters in the world to come to America
and contend for the title of the "best trotter in the world."
During that time, Roosevelt Raceway was busy making
travel reservations for the trainers, drivers, and owners who
had horses that would be competing in the race. Most of
the expenses were generously paid for by Roosevelt.

Another thrill was being permitted inside the Press Box.
It was an honor, for only important people were allowed

to enter. The Press Box at Roosevelt Raceway was unique, for it had the capacity to hold up to two hundred people at one time, who would be seated on two levels. Sitting in the first row would be Fred Epervary (aka Epie) who was the official press box steward. Epervary's job was to keep all the statistics in a race. Next to Epervary would be Mike Lee, who was known as the "Dean of the Press Box" and who happened to be the father of the track announcer, Jack E. Lee. Sitting to the right of Lee was Howie Fensterstock, who had the job of charting the races. There were several other regulars who served as Roosevelt's public relation men. They were Lou Barasch (aka Tootie), Joey Goldstein, Clyde Hirt, Les Wagner, and Barry Lefkowitz- all who were well respected, brilliant PR men.

Conveniently located inside the press box was a "betting window" for those who were there and wished to make a bet. The only problem with the betting window was that there was a "regular" who constantly hogged the window, making others nervously wait, hoping to not get shut out.

One columnist (a man named Henry Hecht) who worked for the *New York Post* was often seen there, but was not liked by the drivers. In one of his stories, he wrote that trainer/driver Billy Hudson "had his pajamas on at the quarter, and was asleep at the half!"

On any normal day in the press box, there would be seven or eight reporters from the *New York Daily News*, a man named Warren Pack from the *New York Journal American* who was known as "one of the best journalists," and Tony Sisti, the handicapper for *Newsday*. During the times when the Messenger or the International Trot took place, the press box would be filled with as many as forty or fifty people, all hoping to be the first to obtain information "straight from the horses' mouth." The publicity department and the press box at Roosevelt Raceway was certainly the busiest for events like the Messenger and the International. You would find Lew Barasch (the director) and Kay Cisco (the secretary) walking around inside the press box. Lou Miller, the former sportswriter and horse trainer, was on hand to add valuable assistance in writing press releases. And although she wasn't officially a part of the staff, Grace "Bunny" Barasch (Lew's wife) would help invaluably during the festivities. The International Trot was the highlight of the year, starting from the minute the race days were approved by the state, to the day the actual race took place. It was the publicity department's responsibility to select the horses that would compete in the race, to make sure the travel arrangements were made, and to promote the event to the highest.

Let's Get The Party Started

There's no doubt about it, during that time of year when the world-class races occurred, millions of people who had been waiting all year long were elated. But after the race was over and the victor was named, the excitement didn't end. For there were many parties that took place: some were private, and others were open to the public. Being invited to the parties for the international races was a dream come true. It was as exciting as waking up on Christmas morning—anticipating what gifts you might find wrapped under the tree.

Those "special" parties were held at magnificent mansions. Underneath bright tents, on perfectly groomed lawns, were tables adorned with beautiful white lace linens and shiny silver place settings. The ambiance was unparalleled. Situated in the center of the lawn was a pond surrounded by magnificent weeping willows. The families of swans that called the lagoon home could be seen bathing or just frolicking with their young cygnets.

The fortunate select people who were invited to these parties would come "dressed to impress." Roosevelt Raceway owner George Morton Levy often attended the parties accompanied by his beautiful daughter, CeCe. The parties would normally begin in the afternoon and last into the late evening hours. But for those who were not as fortunate to be invited to the exclusive parties, they invented their own.

There were several different places where people would go to "let their hair down" and boogey the night away. Some people would go to the Gam Wah, and others to Mimmo's. Other popular places where people would party after the races were the Cherrystone Inn, the Island Inn, the Banjo Inn, the Greentree Inn, the Brass Monkey, Apple Annies, Wheatley Hills Tavern, Julio Cesare, the Americana (Archie Niles' place), Peppy's (Billy Myer's place), or a dive called Footsies.

The stories that took place at these legendary locations are nostalgic and timeless.

₧₧

One night the Gam Wah hosted an event for a charity. Trade Martin and his Band would be entertaining the crowd that evening. At that time, Trade Martin had a million-dollar-a-year contract with Pepsi Cola for writing and performing all of their songs, which were being used for commercials. After they performed their sets, as the band members were getting ready to pack up their equipment, driver Ben Webster went up and generously offered the band leader a $100 tip for their quality performance. Benny loved the music and asked if they would play for another hour. (Webster didn't know that the band was extremely popular and successful already.) Trade (the band leader) politely thanked Benny and told him that although he would love to, he had to decline for the band had an early morning flight to Las Vegas for a two-week booking!

Another amusing story many people remember was the one about a man who owned a bar called the Maple Manor. The owner, a man named Sam, was a rebel and a hell raiser who loved to pull pranks on others and have fun. Sam was friends with all the other bar owners in town. He would regularly visit their places where he would drink shots and then smash the glasses on the floor. One night after the races, Sam along with some of his friends stopped in several other bars in town. By the night's end, the rowdy crew had visited a handful of establishments where they had left dozens of broken shot glasses shattered on the floor. Several weeks later, the disgruntled bar owners got together and visited Sam's place, the Maple Manor. As they began smashing everything in sight—the chairs, the tables, and the glasses, the bartender called the owner to come right over. When Sam arrived, he laughed and joined in. "Payback's a bitch!" he said.

15

A Divorce and a Death

Levy, Nick Grande and Alvin Weil

George Morton Levy

"When you've come to the end of the rope, tie a
knot in it and hold on."

—Unknown

I guess you could say it was a lengthy, profitable, and most
of the time exciting marriage. After all, being together for
over twenty-five years and spending almost every day (and
most nights) with one another can take a toll on anyone.
George Morton Levy and Alvin Weil were together when
Roosevelt Raceway was created. Together, they watched
it grow and develop into one of the most famous harness
tracks in the world. So what happened to this marriage?
Like 60 percent of all marriages, it ended in divorce. It is

said that the main reason for the break-up was because of a corporate struggle. In May, 1967, Weil resigned and left on "not so good" terms. Alvin Weil stepped down as president of Roosevelt Raceway over what he said were "differences between myself and several of my associates on the executive committee." He said these differences had existed for some time. With his departure, Weil promised not to open any other tracks within 200 mile radius. But it didn't take long before Weil reneged on the deal. Alvin Weil and Nicholas A. Grande (vice-president and general manager of the Suffolk Meadows Quarter Horse Association, Inc., and who once worked at Roosevelt Raceway) signed an agreement in 1969, which stated that they agreed to offer each other, at cost, 25 per-cent of any racing stock or stock in a racing-related company that either might acquire for a five-year period ending November 15, 1974. After Weil became president of Roosevelt Raceway in 1960, he made Grande a vice-president. Weil held his position of president of Roosevelt for seven years until Levy let it be known that he was not happy with certain aspects of Weil's decision to back up a track officer suspected of feathering his own nest. (It is said that the man he was talking about was Grande.)

Characteristically, George Morton Levy displayed no bitterness and arranged for Weil to sell his stock for almost $1,000,000. Levy even arranged for Weil a severance deal to keep his friend on the track payroll for the next ten years, at $37,500 a year. Shortly thereafter, plans were being made to open a quarterhorse racetrack. After making the preparations for Parr Meadows (as it would be called) in Yaphank, LI, New York, Weil headed to Florida to live. On the evening of September 22, 1974, while Weil was walking his two dogs outside the condominium where he lived with his wife, a man walked up to him and shot him. The bullet went through his hand (with which he was trying to protect himself) and lodged into his brain. A neighbor saw one of Weil's dogs running loose and contacted his wife who found him lying in a pool of blood in the driveway. While walking the dogs, Weil was clothed in his pajamas, and was wearing an expensive gold watch and a diamond ring. The police ruled out robbery, for there was nothing taken off of his body. They speculated he had been executed "gangland style." The theory apparently was advanced when it was established from powder burns on Weil's face that Weil had been shot at point-blank range from a distance of about eighteen inches. After the shooting, police began digging into a tangled web of romantic and business involvement in connection with the murder. They conducted an investigation on the theory of a gangland killing, for back in the fifties when Weil was an employee of Roosevelt Raceway, part of his job was to retrieve "gangster tainted" stock. The police also investigated a complicated marital past that included five marriages, four divorces, and an "alleged" mistress to whom Weil had supposedly been paying $5,100 a year to. After Weil's murder, the police retained Grande's phone log at Suffolk Meadows where multiple calls were made to him by Weil from Florida. Their interest in Grande was piqued due to a *Newsday* interview.

Mrs. Weil told the authorities that, shortly before her husband was killed, Weil had told her about the contract and said, "If anything happens to me, don't forget the agreement." She said that Weil had just read a *Newsday* article on Grande's $150,000 annual consulting fee from the track (Suffolk Meadows) and said, "He's (Grande) taking money from the track that doesn't belong to him."

Among the many tragedies that had befallen George Levy through the eighty plus years of his life, it is said that only a few hurt him more than the departure of his protégé, friend, and "almost son," Alvin Weil. To this day the murder of Alvin Weil remains a mystery and unsolved. The police stated that they believed it was a "mob" hit, but could never prove it. Ironically, the track Weil invested in- and never got the opportunity to open and stage a race. Meanwhile, Alvin Weil was subpoenaed by the Suffolk County grand jury, for they were investigating business connections of Grande and other track licenses. Of course, Weil never made the court date, for he had been "rubbed out." (As police officials called it.)

Probably Alvin Weil is most remembered by an incident that happened when he was president at Roosevelt Raceway in 1963. On November 8 of that year, a riot broke out at the track after management declared the sixth race official, although only two of the eight horses finished the race due to an accident. About five hundred angry fans smashed the tote board, battled the police, set fires, and caused damage estimating at $30,000. Weil was also cited by the French and Italian governments for his role in popularizing the famous Roosevelt International race. Alvin Weil's "unsolved" death has had many different versions of what may have happened on the night of October 22, 1974, but they are all speculative.

In late 1966, Levy and Johnson sold their stock to San Juan Racing Association at triple the market value. A few months later, in 1967, Weil resigned and sold his share of the racetrack for a little under a million dollars. After Weil stepped down, Levy took over Weil's position as president and worked under the San Juan Racing Association

Executive Committee. In 1970, Levy regained control of the track from the San Juan Racing Association. He was totally in charge but worked under the new owners of Madison Square Gardens. Although he did not own as much stock as he once did, Levy's main objective and goal remained the same- to keep his beloved racetrack at the high standards it had been for the past twenty-seven years. But unfortunately for various reasons, harness racing started to decline. In his final years as the "Father of Roosevelt Raceway" Levy would face crisis after crisis from several new competitors.

These came in the form of OTB and the state lotteries, stockholders discontents, horsemen and union strikes, rumors of "race fixing," escalating taxation of the track, and the last and most likely straw that broke the camel's back was the opening of the state-of-the-art Meadowlands Racetrack which was located in Meadowlands, New Jersey. When Levy saw that he couldn't win the battle against OTB, he surrendered and Roosevelt Raceway was the first track to accept it.

In 1977, George Morton Levy, founder and president of Roosevelt Raceway and pioneer of modern night harness racing, died of a heart attack. He was eighty-nine years old. This brilliant genius, and clairvoyant, who had a vision— and made that vision come true—will be remembered by many for different reasons. In 1939, only the gutsy Levy had the clout to circumvent Nassau County gambling laws and start a dog track. Levy was an elegant businessman who was humorously called "the Marrying Man" by his friends for he tried his hand at it four times. He was an acquaintance and friend to mobsters and pols, first grabbing national limelight by unsuccessfully defending the mobster and "Dope King" Charles "Lucky" Luciano, against white slavery charges brought by New York's future governor, Thomas E. Dewey.

And probably, most of all, was that Levy and his partner invested about $100,000 transforming Vanderbilt Racecourse into what would later become the nation's premier harness racetrack—Roosevelt Raceway.

Some people remember him as the 5-foot 5-inch man who loved smoking Havana cigars, others as the person who founded the premiere races in the world- The Messenger and The Roosevelt Trot- and yet others would remember him as the man who turned harness racing into the best sport in the world.

To George Morton Levy: Thank you for everything you did for the sport of harness racing. There will never be another like you!

Part VI

Levy standing in front of Roosevelt Raceway

The sell out

16

A Change of Ownership

"Leadership is a potent combination of strategy
and character. But if you must be without one, be
without strategy."

—Norman Schwarzkopf

After George Morton Levy's death, harness racing
continued at Roosevelt Raceway for the next eleven years.
In 1984, the track was bought out by Roosevelt Raceway
Associates. But without Levy's parental love and proper
guidance of his 'baby', attendance at Roosevelt declined,
ticket sales could hardly supply its daily operating costs, and
many of the top drivers, trainers, and horses re-located to
the neighboring state-of-the-art Meadowlands Racetrack.

The very last race at Roosevelt was contested on June
15, 1988, when a pacer named Majestic Andrew shared a
$5,500 purse before an announced crowd of a mere 3,054
spectators. The residents of Long Island and millions of
horsemen sadly had to accept the death of not one, but
two important factors that established harness racing into
one of the best sports in the world: the death of George
Morton Levy and the death of Roosevelt Raceway.

Before demolition

During demolition

17

Promises, Lies, and Betrayal

"Each betrayal begins with trust."

—Unknown

It came as a shock to millions of people around the world. Roosevelt Raceway, the first track in the nation to have night-time harness racing was closing its doors. No longer would bettors rush to the windows when the marshal called the horses to the gate. No longer would crowds, which at one time amassed to fifty thousand, run to the rail to cheer for their favorite driver. The track had been bought out by a group of businessmen who said they intended to re-condition it and keep the track going for the horsemen, bettors, and the millions who called Roosevelt Raceway home.

Ten months after Roosevelt Raceway was closed, the grandstand at the once-premier harness track on Long Island was crumbling, its three principal owners were being investigated for possible financial irregularities, and critics said the owners may reap more than $100 million in profits after acquiring the track chiefly through tax breaks. Race-horse owners and unions representing former employees at the tracks said that the owners misled the town of Hempstead by promising to keep the track open if the town supported the raceway purchase through tax-exempt municipal bonds.

Critics said the investors then allowed the track to deteriorate to discourage attendance and to justify selling the 172-acre site, which would now be worth at least $1 million an acre if developed commercially. The new owners denied any wrongdoing in the purchase of the track with publicly assisted financing on later financial reports to regulatory agencies. Hempstead officials said the financial aid was given to the investors as the only way to save the faltering raceway, a thousand jobs, and about $20 million a year that the track pumped into the local economy.

The Nassau County District Attorney's office and New York state and federal officials started investigating separate issues, such as:

1. Did the owners misrepresent their financial ability to operate a racetrack and alter the track's land value to qualify for financing through the Hempstead Town Industrial Development Agency?
2. In 1984, the agency approved a $54 million bond issue that permitted the owners to buy the track and pay off the bonds through interest rates that saved the owners about $2 million a year.
3. Did the investors bring in a race-track expert named David A. Stevenson, as an original partner to bolster their administrative credibility, and then pressure him to sell his $50 investment for $150,000 soon after the bond deal was approved?

4. His $50 investment might have been worth as much as $5 million to the remaining partners, real estate experts said.
5. Did the owners underpay state parimutuel taxes?
6. Did the new owners, after acquiring the track, seek improper tax deductions by inflating the value of the track's buildings and equipment, while claiming steep reductions in the value of the track's land?
7. Officials of unions and racehorse owners said that the track's new owners bought it primarily as a real estate venture, that they neglected maintenance, and, had even closed down the choice seating areas.

"From being one of the best tracks in the country, in a matter of a couple of years it became a hellhole," said Joseph Faraldo, president of the Standardbred Owners Association, a group representing 2,500 owners, trainers, and drivers of harness race horses.

The closing of Roosevelt Raceway, which at one time was the most beautiful and exciting racetrack in the country, meant the loss of a thousand jobs at the track and about nine hundred support jobs surrounding Roosevelt. A groom at the track said, "People who haven't done anything but 'rub' horses all their lives, where are we supposed to go?" But that didn't appear to matter to the new owners. It was all about money and greed!

The many gracious horses that raced over the racetrack, the colorful drivers that entertained the bettors for almost half a century, the track and world records that were made there—were now nothing but a distant memory.

The half-mile racetrack where horses and drivers entertained millions of people is now a condominium complex called Meadowbrook Commons. The asphalt parking lot where millions of people fought for a car space is now a shopping mall and a movie theater. And the area where millions of incredible equine athletes called home is now a Home Depot.

Roosevelt Raceway, once known as the "Taj Mahal" of harness racing, is merely a former shell of itself. The dream and legacy which George Morton Levy founded almost a half century earlier is nothing more than a memory.

The authors of this book are glad Levy is not here to see what became of the billion-dollar legacy that he fought so hard to create and nurture. But in our hearts, there was and always will be only one Roosevelt Raceway: Where It All Began!

The End of a Dynasty

It's hard to believe that it has been almost seventy-five years since a man named George Morton Levy founded what would become one of the greatest sports in history— nighttime harness racing. The genius criminal attorney, who represented renowned criminals such as Lucky Luciano, Frank Erickson, and Frank Costello, had a dream and made the dream come true.

Starting out as a modest venture in 1940, the track struggled until 1946 when Phillips perfected "the starting gate," solving the problem of unnecessary and frustrating recalls in a race. After the gate was perfected and the races started on time, the fans were enamored. In the year 1956, there were major renovations done to the track. Soon thereafter it became known as "The Dream Track."

Levy founded a race called the International Trot which drew horses and people from all over the world. In 1960,

Roosevelt peaked when 54,861 fans turned out for the second running of the International Trot.

Roosevelt Raceway was a true leader, the first to use "the starting gate," "race under the lights," and it was the first track to introduce a new exotic wager called "The Twin Double." The Twin Double was created to produce huge payoffs and exhilarating action, which it did. In October, 1963, while an elderly fan was busy filling out paperwork for a $1,683 win, he suffered a heart attack and died at the cashier's window.

Despite several scandals and a few isolated incidents that Roosevelt provided, the track supplied the highest quality racing in its day—like the Messenger Stakes (the first leg in the harness Triple Crown) and the International Trot.

Unforeseen circumstances arose. The first was the opening of the Meadowlands in 1976. In the mid-eighties, OTB stopped paying the racetracks their percentages from the handle. They owed Roosevelt and Yonkers Raceway $25,000,000. Driver/trainer Lucien Fontaine, who was the president of the New York SOA, attempted to collect the money for his fellow horsemen. Shortly after, the state of New York counter-sued Fontaine for $58,000,000, leaving him no choice but to back off for he did not have the funding to fight. On top of that, everyone in the SOA abandoned Fontaine and disassociated themselves from him out of fear that the state would sue them too. The combination of the introduction of OTB (off-track betting), the opening of the Meadowlands, and the death of Roosevelt's founder, George Morton Levy, was too much for the racetrack to bear.

In the year 1984, Roosevelt was sold to new owners with the stipulation that the track would remain open and running. Four years later, the new proprietors announced that they were closing the one and only Roosevelt Raceway. A furor erupted. Lawsuits were flying and people were dragged through the mud, but in the end the track that pleasured millions of people for so many years was gone. Perhaps this was the beginning of things to come, for since then there have been many racetracks around the country to follow in Roosevelt Raceway's steps.

Sadly, the sport of harness racing in many areas has come upon hard times. There are many factors that account for this unfortunate event. While casinos have provided opportunities for some, the competition for the gaming dollar has caused a significant decline in on-track attendance and overall handle on our sport, and particularly hard hit are the states where racing has to stand up on its own "four hooves."

Perhaps the sport of harness racing will someday be back where it began. But one thing for sure is that "real" horsemen will never submit and will continue as their forefathers did back in the beginning of the century. They will get together, put up their own money, and race horses for the love and thrill of the sport.

Perhaps someday in the future our children and grandchildren will get the opportunity to experience the thrill and excitement that money cannot buy, as we did who were lucky enough to have participated in the sport of harness racing. We cannot let our hopes and dreams die, for as George Morton Levy proved to all of us, dreams do come true!

ROOSEVELT RACEWAY   "MAJESTIC ANDREW"   JUNE 15, 1988
LAPARMA STABLE,   -TIME 2:01:3-   R. DAIGNEAULT dr.
S. WEISMAN   J. HOFFMAN tr.
     ORE ELSE WHAT 2nd   CHOCOLATE TOPPING 3rd

Majestic Andrew with Regean Daigneault winning
the last race at Roosevelt June 15, 1988

Book Two

Foreword

I was only seven years old in September 1940 when Roosevelt Raceway opened. My father was Chairman of The New York Racing Commission at the time as well as an active participant in the sport as an owner and amateur driver of a stable of trotters. He was, therefore, involved with Roosevelt Raceway, both from a supervisory standpoint and as an active participant.

While too young to go to the track at night, my early recollections are from what my father told us about the opening meeting. Roosevelt, as we know, revolutionized our sport by initiating pari-mutuel harness racing at night in a major metropolitan area. Naturally something so innovative took time to catch on. Horsemen were reluctant to ship horses in, resulting in short fields, and the necessity to have most horses race two heats to fill a program. My father and his uncle Roland Harriman's Arden Homestead Stable shared the same manager, Billy Dickerson, and to help out, persuaded him to speed up conditioning trotters being primed for later in the season to send them to the opening meet. The result was unexpected purse money started coming to Dickerson to the extent he angrily thought Roland had sold the horses without his approval.

An interesting incident occurred in the early days regarding photo finishes. According to my father, prior to the establishment of a photo finish camera, the judges would post the results as they saw them. When a camera was finally developed and installed, there was often a delay in developing the film and posting the results as they saw them and payout machines were opened.

One night my father received a call in the commissioner's box that the judges had posted the wrong order of a particular close finish, and tellers were already paying off on the previously posted results. Sensing trouble, my father rushed to the room where photo finishes were developed; intercepted the runner responsible for posting the photo for public display and probably prevented a riot from disgruntled bettors. Yes, he let the incorrect results become official. The judges were read the riot act and instructed never again to post results until confirmed by the photo finish camera.

My father went off to war in 1942 serving as an officer in the U.S. Army Air Corp. While he had been granted a leave of absence from The New York State Racing Commission, he had resigned in 1944 when the state decided to not allow horses owned by a Commissioner to race at any New York State track. He returned as an active owner, close friend and mentor to George Morton Levy and others in the high command at Roosevelt Raceway.

Living only 15 minutes from the track, and now a teenager, he and I spent many nights at the track. Those were glorious days for me visiting the paddock with our trainer/driver Harry Pownall, and listening to and standing in awe of people like Henry Thomas, Frank Ervin, Frank Safford, Paul Vineyard, Jimmy Jordan, Del Miller, Sach Werner and so many others.

As I got older, I jogged horses with Gene Pownall and met the two men who came to dominate the sport in the 60's and beyond- Billy Haughton and Stanley Dancer. When the crowds got large, we found a way to get on the roof of the old grandstand with a superb view of the track. I watched the disaster when KAOLA went down in the first turn followed by six or seven others including our own WALTER SPENCER who actually recovered after dumping Harry Pownall, lead for a mile and then pulled himself up.

It was chaos and Henry Thomas never fully recovered from the accident. On another night, I witnessed our own FLORICAN, driven by Harold Miller, win the American Trotting championship, defeating heavy favorite KATIE KEY. We made it from the grandstand roof to the Winners Circle in time to accept the trophy. Then the celebration began.

These were the glorious days for my family and me. Roosevelt Raceway became the mecca of harness racing and the sport flourished thanks to the vision of George Levy and the support of the owners, trainers, and drivers from everywhere.

I appreciate and thank Bill Haughton, Jr. and especially his mother, Dottie, my longtime and dear friend ,for asking me to write about the early days at Roosevelt Raceway. I only wish we could have them back.

—Elbridge "Ebby"T. Gerry, Jr. (owner /trainer/breeder/ amateur driver/trustee emeritus of Harness Racing Museum and Hall of Fame)

For the forty-eight years Roosevelt Raceway was open and undoubtedly the most famous harness track in the country, there were many drivers who came to the half-mile track and within a short time would become celebrities. It was not uncommon to open the *New York Times* and see the name of a harness driver from Roosevelt setting a new track or world record, and yet others for something a little more colorful, such as being involved in a scandal of some kind.

There were hundreds of drivers who deserve gratitude and praise for helping to make Roosevelt the king of all racetracks, but unfortunately we do not have space for everyone. We have listed the top drivers polled from fans and have tried to acknowledge as many as possible. A big thanks goes out to all the drivers who at one time or another pleased the fans by participating in a race there.

"This one's for the boys!"

1

The Legends of Roosevelt (Leading Drivers)

"I'm not the best—but there's nobody better."

—Carmine Abbatiello

In this section we list the top drivers from Roosevelt Raceway who were selected by fans on an online poll. Along with a short bio of each driver, there is a story that is remembered by fellow horsemen that makes each driver special in his own way.

We hope you enjoy this, as we did, for these men were superstars and always will be.

Note: Although today there are many modern day greats, such as Dave Palone, Brian Sears, Tim Tetrick, John Campbell, Yannick Gingras, Cat Manzi, David Miller, Billy O'Donnell, Ron Pierce, Mike Lachance, and many others who have earned higher winning earnings or set more track records than the drivers at Roosevelt, remember back then the purses were much smaller and the racing season was shorter.

L-R Buddy Gilmour, Carmine Abbatiello,
Lucien Fontaine and Del Insko

Stanley Dancer

Stanley Dancer (7/25/27–9/9/05)

Stanley Dancer was the son of a potato/dairy farmer who called New Egypt, New Jersey, his home. In 1946, he began his driving career at Freehold Raceway. For his first race, he borrowed the blue and gold racing silks of Dick Baker. Stanley adopted the colors as his own and, ironically, Dick would end up working for Stanley.

Dancer was known as a man of impeccable honesty and integrity in a sport that depends upon the public's trust. Stanley started out on the bottom as a groom, worked his way to the top, and became one of the premier horsemen in the world.

Dancer was also the guest at the White House of four different presidents.

In the year 1945, at the age of eighteen, Dancer went on his own. He purchased a "broken down" horse called David Guy D for $50, and purchased another horse for an owner. After working religiously with his new purchase, he was able to get David Guy D sound enough to race.

Getting the first thrill of many to come for Dancer, he won his first race with his horse at Freehold in 1946. Although Dancer did a great job in rehabilitating him, he was not able to keep him sound. After the win and the breakdown of David Guy D, the other horse that he had was never able to finish better than fourth, so, reluctantly, he went back to grooming horses for other trainers.

In 1947, his wife (Rachel) was able to come up with $250 to purchase another horse that also had lameness problems. The horse was named Candor. After many hours of tending to his horses problems, Stanley got the horse sound and the horse went on to earn the Dancer's $12,000.

In 1948, after making a deal with then Roosevelt race secretary Walter Gibbons, Stanley started training and driving at Roosevelt Raceway on a trial basis. His style of racing was aggressive and gung ho. He liked going to the front, playing "catch me if you can" with the other drivers and started winning races. This style of racing horses proved extremely successful for Dancer, making him one of the best harness drivers in history of harness racing.

Dancer leased an eight-year-old horse from New Zealand named Cardigan Bay and brought him over to the United States. The horse went to be the first Standardbred pacer to earn $1 million in a career. That was quite a feat in those days!

Dancer was, and always will be, an icon of harness racing. He won the Trotting Triple Crown (two times), with Nevele Pride in 1968 and Super Bowl in 1972. He also won the pacing Triple Crown with Most Happy Fella in 1970.

Throughout his career, he drove the likes of champions, Nevele Pride, Albatross, Su Mac Lad, Super Bowl, Most Happy Fella, Keystone Ore, and many others.

Perhaps the Universal Driver Rating System (UDRS) speaks best for Dancer. Like a .300 batting average in baseball is considered excellent in successive years from 1962–1968, Stanley's UDRS rating was a phenomenal—.468, .468, .442, .423, .493, .488 and .511.

Incomparable statistics!

In the six decades that Stanley raced, he brought excitement, honesty, and integrity to the sport of harness racing.

Stanley Dancer passed away at the age of seventy-eight on September 8, 2005, in his beloved Pompano Beach, Florida. Although he is no longer with us in person, Stanley Dancer's spirit and name will live forever.

Billy Haughton

William R. Haughton (11/23/23–7/15/86)

Billy Haughton was an American harness driver and trainer who is considered one of harness racing's top trainer/drivers.

His peers in the business called him the Master. He won the Hambletonian four times, the Little Brown Jug five times, and he is the *only* driver to win the Messenger Stakes seven times.

With a career record of 4,910 wins and over $40 million in earnings, Haughton was first in annual earnings twelve times—1952–1959,1963,1965,1967, and 1968. In dashes, he won from 1953 to 1958.

"He meant as much to harness racing as Arnold Palmer did to golf, or Babe Ruth did to baseball. Billy was the best all-around horseman in the history of the sport," said fellow horsemen and Hall of Famer Delvin Miller.

Born in Gloversville, New York, Haughton came from a farming background. His first start as a driver came by accident. He was working for Billy Muckle at Saratoga and when Muckle was a no show for a race one day, Haughton went to the judges to report it.

The judge said to him, "Give me $5 for a driver's license" (which Billy did), and he was now a driver. Thus began his lucrative career.

As a youngster, he exercised thoroughbreds at Saratoga Raceway. After realizing he would be too big to be a jockey, he steered his sights toward harness racing: grooming then training and driving harness horses.

In the mid-1940s, he started developing a stable of his own and soon thereafter became the leading driver at Saratoga in 1946. Haughton was the epitome of the "All American" harness driver and trainer. He was handsome, humble, a true gentleman, and passionate about what he did. In the harness world, Billy was known as "America's Sweetheart" because of his genuine kindness and honesty. Haughton would share his knowledge with rivals that he considered friends, and always would take the time to help them with any problems if asked. He always found time for anyone, be it a groom, a child, a racetrack owner, or a fan.

"We shared his friendship, his advice, and his counsel," said Stanley Bergstein, then president of Harness Tracks of America, who had a thirty-five-year friendship with him. "The stakes and the money do not do justice to the man.

He spoke for all of us, and he did it in a way that generated admiration and respect," Bergstein said.

Some of his best horses during his career were Rum Customer, who won the pacing Triple Crown in 1968; and Green Speed, who was named "Harness Horse of the Year" in 1977. Haughton drove Meadow Paige to a world record of 1:55.2 in a time trial at Lexington in 1967. That was unheard of in those days! Other great horses he drove and trained were Belle Acton, Handle with Care, Laverne Hanover, Romulus Hanover, Nihilator, Falcon Almahurst, MacKenzie Almahurst, Cold Comfort, Doublemint, Keystone Pioneer and many others.

It's hard to say how far Billy could have gone and how many world records he would have set if it weren't for his life ending way too early. If Haughton were alive today, some say he would be compared to a combination of Ron Burke (top trainer) and Tim Tetrick (top driver).

At the height of his career, Haughton had a stable of more than two hundred horses, which he managed and raced at various tracks around the country.

One story people remember about Billy is when he was in a race and a driver who should not have been given a license had his horse all over the track. The young man had no clue how to drive a horse and was a hazard on the racetrack. After the race was over, Haughton went up to this young fellow and asked him, "How did you ever get your driver's license?"

The young man responded, "Why, Mr. Haughton, *you* signed for me!"

After that, Haughton made it a point never to sign for anyone again.

In his personal life, Haughton was a great father and husband. His family remembers one time when he was getting on his boat. He slipped on the dock and fell into the water, where half of his ear was cut off and he was unconscious. If it had not been for his wife, Dottie, who held his head above water until help came, he most likely would have drowned. Tragically, on July 15, 1986, Haughton was involved in an accident in a race at Yonkers Raceway.

Billy Haughton died in Valhalla, New York, from head injuries he sustained in the race. At the peak of his career, he was the all-time leading race winner and money earner in the sport.

"The Red Man" Carmine Abbatiello

Carmine Abbatiello (The "Red Man")

Carmine Abbatiello was born on May 23, 1936. He came from Staten Island, New York, and at one time ranked as harness racing's all-time second dash winning driver with more than 7,000 wins.

As soon as he graduated from Staten Island's Port Richmond High, Carmine began apprenticing for his older brother, Anthony. Eight years later, in 1963, young Carmine ventured out and started his own stable. In his first few years of racing, The Red Man (as he would be nicknamed because of his scarlet-colored racing silks) won 104 races and made $211,998 in purses and he won the driving title at Monticello in 1961 and 1963. It took Carmine twenty-eight years to win his five thousandth win, which occurred at Roosevelt Raceway—an achievement that won him a "night at the track."

For his special night, The Red Man was to drive a red Cadillac convertible down the stretch to the winners circle for the ceremony. When they told Carmine to stand in the back of the car and wave to the patrons, he said, "Over my dead body. They'd shoot me. I'll sit in the front, but I don't want to go alone. I want Ted Wing and Jimmy Marohn to go with me." The two other drivers gladly obliged and jumped in the back seat.

Carmine was a fan favorite who became one of the most popular of all sulky drivers on the New York circuit and the first city native to win a driving championship on local tracks. He holds the record for most wins by any driver at Roosevelt Raceway, with 2,575 wins.

Carmine won his seven thousandth race on October 23, 1990, at Yonkers Raceway with a horse appropriately named Right on Course. Abbatiello won driving titles at all of the New York area tracks and became known as "one of the top catch drivers" in the history of harness racing, with annual winnings surpassing $3 million five times, even though throughout his career he never won a race with a purse of $100,000 or greater.

The Hall of Famer won two hundred or more races fifteen times, including 393 in 1979 and 391 in 1980. His annual earnings surpassed $3 million five times.

Carmine is remembered by many as "the master of the one-line wise cracks." When being interviewed by *Sports Illustrated*, the reporter asked Carmine what the difference was between him and the other drivers. Carmine put up two fingers and said, "Two seconds".

Today, Carmine spends his winters in the Florida Keys. During the spring and summer, he can be found in New Jersey helping his son Eric with the training of his stable.

Jimmy Cruise on Kash Minbar

Jimmy Cruise (10/12/17–1/30/02)

Jimmy Cruise was a second-generation horseman. He started racing his father's horses on the Indiana/Kentucky fair circuit while still in high school. He called everyone "partner" and was one of the most respected trainers in the business.

Because of his ability to diagnose lameness in horses, his peers called him a genius. He once sold a trotter to a gentleman for $500. The next day, the guy came back with the horse and told Jimmy that he sold him a lame horse. Jimmy reached in his pocket and gave the man his money back. Cruise took the horse, Earl Laird, back into his stable. The horse would go on to become one of the best trotters in the country.

On July 12, 1958, Jimmy became the first driver to win six parimutuel races on one program at any track in the

US or Canada—and he did it at Roosevelt Raceway. That night he had six mounts entered to race—all from his own stable—and he won all of them. Before the races, Cruise thought that he could win with all of his mounts, so he had Clint Hodgins' young assistant trainer, Lucien Fontaine, place some bets for him. He bet each horse individually, not as a par-lay.

Jimmy won with the first two and started to think that he should call his bets off on the others so he sent a friend up to the grandstand to find Lucien and stop him from betting the other horses. In the meantime, Jimmy wins another race. His friend came back and told him that he was unable to find Lucien. Again, he sent his friend back out to find Lucien but could never locate him. That night Cruise went on to win the rest of his races—and since no one could find Lucien and he bet all six horses for Jimmy, he won all his bets.

From the 1950s through the 1970s, Cruise was one of the dominant trainer/drivers at Yonkers and Roosevelt Raceway. In all, Jimmy would win four driving championships (more than 1700 races) and $6 million in his career.

During his reign, Cruise twice represented the United States in the International Trot at Roosevelt Raceway, with the horse Kash Minbar.

Cruise had a special talent of figuring out ailments on a horse that the other trainers could not. Thus, he was nicknamed by his fellow horsemen "The Doctor." A journalist once wrote, "Jimmy Cruise can take some spit, tape, glue, and turn a lame horse into a free-for-aller."

Several top horses campaigned by Cruise were Earl Laird, Express Rodney, Stormy Dream, Frank T. Ace and Mr. Budlong. Sadly, Jimmy Cruise passed away on January 30, 2002.

Buddy Gilmour

William "Buddy" Gilmour 7/23/32–5/22/11

Probably one of the most controversial drivers in the history of harness racing was a man named William "Buddy" Gilmour. Many times in his career, he would make the front pages of the newspapers for incidents other than winning stake races, including accusations of race fixing, tax evasion, and the famous "Superfecta Trial."

Outside of these unfortunate incidents, Buddy was described by many as "one of the best drivers in the sport." As a human being, they didn't come any better. If someone was having financial difficulties, Buddy was the first to offer assistance.

There was a time when another driver/trainer was having financial difficulties. Buddy sold one of his own horses and got $8,000 for him. A few days later, Gilmour came into the locker room with the money that he had gotten for selling the horse. Gilmour graciously gave all the money to the trainer to pay off his debts.

Off the track, Buddy loved to have a good time. One night while he has at a local club called the Gam Wah, he entered followed by a Dixieland jazz band playing the song "When the Saints Come Marching In." The band members were all dressed in red and white striped vests and wore old-fashioned straw hats. Buddy had hired the band for the night and their job for the evening was to follow him around from club to club, playing their music as he would enter each club.

Buddy was also known as a very generous tipper. $100 tips were the norm with him and many times he would pick up the checks of friends when out dining.

He was born in Lucan, Ontario, in 1932, and knew early on in his life that harness racing was what he wanted to do. Buddy apprenticed under Hall of Famer Clint Hodgins. After leaving Clint, he started driving on the Buffalo-Batavia circuit, until 1962, when he tragically lost his entire eighteen-horse stable in a barn fire at Batavia Downs. The loss included two of his best horses, Howard Rosecroft and Demon Damsel. After the devastation, Buddy uprooted his family and moved to start anew at Roosevelt Raceway. That choice would turn out to be a very successful and lucrative one. With that move it was recorded that Gilmour had $1 million-plus seasons fifteen times.

Some of his best mounts were On the Road Again, Follow My Star, Joie De Vie, Mirror Image, Steinam, and Millers Scout.

The Gilmour name was a familiar one in the harness horse industry. Buddy was one of four brothers in the business who drove, the others being Lloyd, George, and John.

In 1992, Buddy Gilmour semi-retired. Eleven years later, in 2003, he hung up his colors for good after forty successful years. Sadly, harness racing lost another legend on May 22, 2011, when Gilmour died at the age of seventy-eight.

Drivers John Chapman, George Sholty,
Billy Haughton, Del Insko, Herve Filion,
Clint Hodgins, Del Miller and Stanley Dancer

John Chapman

John Chapman (11/25/28–5/2/80)

John Chapman is described by many as "one of the best catch drivers during the golden age of trotting" at harness tracks Yonkers and Roosevelt Raceway. John began his career in 1947 at the age of nineteen. His forte was having a light touch and a hard will. But it wasn't all easy sailing for Chapman. Throughout his life, he had to overcome many adversities.

The first was the devastation of a barn fire which wiped out his entire stable, and the second was fighting a mysterious and debilitating illness.

During his career, John would drive 3,915 winners and his horses would earn $21,359,746. In the year 1969 alone,

Chapman would drive 197 winners and have winnings of $1,063,746.

Probably his most famous drive was in steering Delmonica Hanover first across the finish line in the $150,000 International Trot at Roosevelt Raceway in 1973.

He repeated that feat with Delmonica one year later in the 1974 edition of the International-that on with a purse of $200,000.

Chapman had a bad habit of smoking. No one has any idea how many cigarettes he would smoke per day. He loved to smoke. His friends recall as Chappie would get in his bike to race horses, he would flick his cigarette onto the track.

One time while he was racing at Buffalo, he was thrown from the bike and landed in the lap of driver Ed Arthur. As the startled driver started to ease up (with Chappie sitting in his lap), Chapman yelled out to him "What are you doing? We still have a shot at third!" and third they finished.

One day, on May 2, 1980, Chapman was qualifying a horse at Roosevelt Raceway. The horse was a bad actor and was pulling his "guts out". When John got off of the bike, he was as white as a ghost. He told another driver as he entered the locker room, "Boy, that one really got me."

John Chapman went home, and later that afternoon died of a heart attack.

Benny "The Whip" Webster

Benny "The Whip" Webster

Unfortunately, as it is in most sports, when it comes to harness racing all news is not positive. Many times this famous harness driver would make the front page of the newspapers. Unfortunately, it wouldn't be for winning races; it would be for false allegations of race fixing. But negative publicity was but a tiny notch in Benny's belt.

Benny "The Whip" grew up in Hilton, New York, dreaming that one day he might win a Hambletonian and a Little Brown Jug. And that's exactly what this natural did.

Along with several other great drivers—Carmine Abbatiello, John Chapman, Buddy Gilmour, and Billy Haughton—Benny would certainly have his name go down in the history books. In the year 1976, Webster purchased a horse from Stanley Dancer named Oil Burner.

The horse went on to win the Oliver Wendell Holmes and The Monticello-OTB Classic, which at that time was the richest race in harness racing, with a purse of $300,000. Shortly after, the horse was syndicated for $2.7 million. (Remember, this was over thirty-seven years ago!)

But probably his claim to fame was when he purchased a horse named Flak Bait. One day while looking at horses that were consigned in a horse sale, he spotted a horse that he "just had to have." He loved the looks of the horse but didn't have the money to purchase him. He was determined to buy the horse for he had a gut feeling about the colt. The night before the horse sale, the gutsy Webster went to a casino with $500 and luckily made enough money ($70,000 at the baccarat table) to buy the colt.

The rest is history. Flak Bait went on to win the 1985 Kentucky Futurity. The horse earned Benny $90,000 as a two-year-old, over $1,000,000 as a three-year-old, and then was syndicated for $4,000,000. When Webster retired in 2004, he had amassed 4,378 wins and made over $43,197,645 in purse earnings!

Benny "The Whip" had one of the most colorful lives and was well loved by his fans. One time, Benny "the prankster" hired a streaker to run across the track at Roosevelt Raceway. As the naked lady crossed the track with everyone's eyes glued to her, Benny was waiting in the getaway car.

Today, Benny is retired and living in up state New York.

Del Insko

Del Insko 7/10/31-

Delmer (Del) M. Insko was born on July 10, 1931, in Amboy, Minnesota. Del was one of the more dominate harness drivers at New York's Roosevelt and Yonkers Raceway's in the 1960s and 1970s.

A memorable night in 1966 would put Insko on the map, when he drove a trotter named Speedy Rodney to a 1:58.3 mile at Yonkers, which set a track record and would hold up for almost eighteen years!

In 1975, Insko achieved another amazing feat when he swept through Roosevelt's International Trotting Series, winning all three races with a horse named Savoir.

Five years later, he accomplished what he called "the biggest thrill in racing"—his win in the $2 million Woodrow Wilson Pace at the Meadowlands with Land Grant.

In the history of harness racing, there have only been two races with a purse of two million or greater. (At that time, the Woodrow Wilson was the richest race in the world for both harness and thoroughbred racing.)

Del began his racing career in 1946, by driving in the mid-west, and, in 1950, he was driving along with his father at Laurel Racetrack in Maryland. In 1960, he became the youngest driver ever to win a North American Dash-winning championship.

In 1950, tragedy struck the Insko family when Del lost two sisters and a brother who were killed in a terrible accident. (Their car was hit by a train crossing railroad tracks coming home from a party.)

Throughout his career, Del had a career best of 306 wins in a year (second in the country) and had 200 or more victories nine straight years through 1973. Insko is remembered by many as "the driver who always had a toothpick in his mouth." He was nicknamed "Mr. Resilience" because of the many accidents he was involved in, and many times the doctors had told him that he would never race again (They were wrong). Insko would certainly have had more than the 5,000 wins that he is credited with if he had driven on Mondays. Being a family man, it was his policy that every Sunday he would fly home to his farm in Illinois where he would spend quality time with his wife and children.

Back home he would look after the farm horses and the Chicago racing stable that his brother Delbert ran for him. After spending time with his family, he would return to New York on either Tuesday or Wednesday.

Today, Del Insko is enjoying retirement with his wife (Bonnie) at their farm in Illinois.

Lucien "Loosh" Fontaine

Lucien "Loosh" Fontaine 4/12/39-

Probably one of the most respected and likable men in harness racing is a man named Lucien Fontaine (aka Loosh).

Lucien would always tell people "I can get speed out of any horse." And he did!

At the age of fourteen, Fontaine was driving a milk wagon, and by the young age of fifteen he began working for legendary horseman Keith Waples in Canada.

While working for Waples, Lucien observed horses racing that were beating the best Canadian horses. Lucien asked, "Where did those horses come from?" He was told that the horses came from America.

One day, a driver came to Canada to race. As they paraded this driver around, the fans and the track made a big deal of him. Loosh asked, "Who is that guy and where did he come from?" He was told that the man was Buddy Gilmour and he came from America. After seeing the American horses and Buddy Gilmour, Loosh said, "I must go there."

That year, Fontaine joined the Clint Hodgins stable and was on his way to the United States. (Clint was the trainer of the great pacer Bye Bye Byrd.) He arrived at Roosevelt Raceway in 1957 where he worked for Hodgins as a second trainer. Loosh says it took him longer to get from Yonkers to Roosevelt than it did for him to get to Yonkers from Canada.

In 1960, Clint sent Lucien to Rockingham Park with two of his maiden homebreds. He told Fontaine if he didn't win any races not to bother coming back. While at Rockingham Park, Fontaine not only won one race, he won many and Hodgins summoned him back to Roosevelt.

He got his first Roosevelt Raceway drive in 1960 when his mentor put him down on a horse that was in to go. The horse's name was Carmita Hanover, who had post position number 8. The young, confident Lucien looked at the program and told Clint that he thought he could win the race. Clint looked at him funny and said, "Do you have a fever or something? Get out there and get beat like the rest of us."

But the ambitious young man came from behind to win the race and lit up the tote board, paying $72.00 to win.

Fontaine is known and credited for many things including the following:

1. He never wore driving gloves—no matter how cold it was outside.
2. He was voted by the fans as their most favorite driver—receiving more than six thousand votes.
3. Lucien Fontaine is known as the "father of the modern day driver."

In 1964, Lucien quit training horses and became a full-time driver, setting the pace for future "catch" drivers.

He has done much work behind the scenes, including having the driver and trainer percentages being paid directly from the track—as opposed to the old system of monies earned for driving and training being paid to the owner, who then dispersed it to the driver/trainer.

Throughout his career, Fontaine drove 175 or more winners nine times. His best year was in 1968 when he had an unbelievable 264 winners in 1,359 starts. At that time, Loosh was second in the nation to Herve Filion in winners, and fourth in earnings with $1,077,251.

During his racing career, Lucien won over $1 million a year ten times. Loosh is probably best known for driving and training a horse named Forrest Skipper, who was the Horse of the Year in 1986. As a four-year–old, the horse went undefeated in sixteen starts and earned Fontaine a million-dollar bonus.

Other great horses he drove or trained were Valiant Bret, Country Don, Irish Napoleon, Shadow Rocket, Big Towner, Pocomoonshine, Cigar Store Injun, Rumpus Hanover, WW Smith, Hodgin Special, Tropic Song, and Oscar RL.

Some of his more memorable wins were the Breeders Crown, US Pacing Championship, the Messenger, Dan

Patch Pace, Graduate Pace Final, Driscoll, Oliver Wendell Holmes, and many New York Sire Stake Finals.

Unfortunately, Fontaine's career ended prematurely in 1989 due to open heart surgery. The name Lucien Fontaine is known by millions worldwide as "one of the best harness drivers." Because of his keen eye on choosing top young horses, Fontaine is often seen at horse sales, checking out potential prospects for clients and friends.

Today, Loosh enjoys going to Pompano Park Racetrack where he lives and is still actively involved in the harness industry.

Carmine Abbatiello, Eldon Harner and
Norman Dauplaise in a race

George Sholty

George Sholty (11/02/32–12/16/2000)

George Sholty was a Hall of Fame harness driver, trainer, and winner of more than $20 million in purse money. He won his first race in 1951, when he started out racing in the mid-west.

Sholty won the Maywood driving title twice before moving his racing operation to the East Coast (Roosevelt Raceway) in 1958. Sholty started working with trainer Gene Sears, who was the grandfather of Brian Sears. Later, he went to work for Tommy Winn, where he got his big break when Tommy was in an accident and was sidelined for a year.

Sholty was one of the dominant drivers of his era, winning numerous titles at Yonkers and Roosevelt Raceway in New York. He had a great sense of humor and the patience of a saint.

One racing night, a fan who was hanging over the rail was cursing at Sholty all night long. When George left the paddock, this same man was standing in the parking lot, still cursing at him. Sholty walked up to him and asked, "How much money did you bet on me?"

The disgruntled fan replied, "Twenty dollars."

Sholty reached in his pocket, pulled out a twenty dollar bill, handed it to the man, and said, "Never bet on me again."

In all, Sholty would win 2,934 races and earn $20,777,666 in purse money. In 1966, he shared in winning the Pacing Triple Crown with Billy Myer. At that time, they shared the driving duties of Romeo Hanover.

He was not only a great driver but a very successful trainer, with champions such as Coffee Break, Conifer, Gentle Stroke, Express Ride, Anniecrombie, Armbro Fling, Rivaltime, Scott S. Hanover, Passing Glance, Ideal Society, and Raven Hanover.

Some of his victories included the 1979 Hambletonian with Legend Hanover, the 1979 Meadowlands Pace with Sonsam, and three Breeders Crown races—with Conifer in 1984, Express Ride in 1985, and Armbro Fling in 1987.

George Sholty's last drive in a race was in 1998.

Herve Filion

Herve Filion 2/1/40–

On February 1, 1940, a baby boy was born in Angers, Quebec, who one day would become one of the most famous harness drivers in the world. His name is Herve Filion. He was the son of a harness driver and the brother of seven other harness drivers.

Herve Filion would be the first driver to win over four hundred races in a year and amazingly was able to achieve this accomplishment fourteen more times. He is also the first driver to win 15,000 races in his lifetime.

Filion grew up on a farm. His love for horses started as a young child. His father began racing harness horses as a hobby when Herve was nine. While he was in school, he would run home every day at lunchtime to work with the horses and then run back to school. Herve quit school after the fifth grade, and, at thirteen, began driving and winning professionally.

He won his first horse race at the young age of thirteen, even though he could barely reach the stirrups.

Filion was rightfully inducted into the Canadian and United States Harness Racing Hall of Fames in the year 1976. Herve won the "Harness Driver of the Year" award ten times in the first twenty-two years it was presented.

When hearing the name Herve Filion, many people remember the time when he stood up on the seat of the race bike, holding the reins with one hand as he paraded before the grandstand.

Not only was Herve an excellent horseman but he was also a showman who was loved by millions.

Herve set the pace for the modern day driver by being the first to drive at multiple tracks which he began doing in the 1960s. He would race at Freehold during the day and then race in the evenings either at Liberty Bell or Brandywine. In the 1970s, his evening schedule changed to Roosevelt Raceway or Yonkers.

Filion officially retired in October 2012 (on his seventieth birthday) after his final win at Rideau Carleton Racetrack in Ottawa. Herve ended his remarkable career with a record of 15,180 wins.

Joe O'Brien

Joe "Jigglin' Joe" O'Brien (6/25/17–9/1984)

Joe O'Brien was one of the all-time greats in harness racing. Those who watched Joe O'Brien drive in a race always waited to see his "signature" way of driving. The Canadian Hall of Famer had a way of jiggling the lines, urging the trotters and pacers he drove, at the most critical moments in the race. On the racetrack, his style of racing was to see how close he could come to another driver without touching them.

"Little Joe" was born in Alberton, Prince Edward Island, on June 25, 1917. He was regarded as one of the premier all-round horsemen in the sport with his legacy preserved by the O'Brien Awards. (The O'Brien Awards are Canada's highest honors.)

Jiggling Joe began his career as a harness driver at the young age of thirteen. At the age of eighteen, he left his home to pursue his career. He started out his career in Maine, where he met trainer George Phalen. The two men quickly became lifetime friends. While O'Brien won over four thousand races and his horses earned more than $20 million, it is not the cold statistics that cover his contribution to the development of harness racing.

The USTA Guide Book needs three pages of compact type to cover his amazing biography, race records, and list of classic races won.

Some of the highlights in his racing career were winning the Little Brown Jug with Shadow Wave and Melvins Woe; the Maple Leaf Trot with Flower Child and Ima Lula; the Cane Pace with Nero, and the Kentucky Futurity with Safe Mission, Governor Armbro, Arnie Almahurst and Armbro Flight. He won the Roosevelt International Trot twice and steered Steady Star to a world record of 1:52 in a time trial.

O'Brien wrote the section on equipment in the book *The Care and Training of the Trotter and Pacer.* When he was asked why he didn't list a piece of equipment in the book that he used all the time, he said, "If I told them everything, they would end up knowing more than me."

Before Joe O'Brien died in 1984, he served as director of the USTA and president of the California Breeder's Association.

Wayne "Curly" Smart

Wayne "Curly" Smart 8/29/04-11/14/76

Another outstanding great name in harness racing is Wayne "Curly" Smart. He began driving at Roosevelt Raceway in the mid 1940s and spent over fifty years in the harness racing industry. He was an outstanding horseman and was known as one of the best drivers in the business.

Smart was cofounder of the world-famous Little Brown Jug, the most prestigious three-year-old pacing race in North America. Back in 1946, Curly won the very first Little Brown Jug with the horse Ensign Hanover.

In the early days, Smart had twenty-one 2:00 performers, which was quite an accomplishment at that time. (This was a time when races were going in 2:10.) Meadow Rice carried Curly to his second Jug winner in 1952.

Among his claims to fame were Scottish Pence, Gold Worthy, Scotch Harbour, and Milestone.

Curly was known as "canny, resourceful and bold" by his fellow drivers.

Henry Thomas with actor James Cagney

Henry Thomas

Thomas was one of the originals to race at Roosevelt Raceway, and one of the few old timers who were able to make the transition over to having to obey and follow the racing rules. He won the driving title at Roosevelt Raceway in 1948 and 1951.

In recalling some of the earlier drivers of the past, no one could claim a more colorful pedigree than horseman Thomas.

He would become famous by some of his racing moves. It is said that whenever Henry would get "boxed in," he would shift his weight in the sulky so as to bump the driver and horse beside him into the next lane, so he could get out.

Another one of his tricks that he liked to do was when he got alongside another driver, he would grab the arch of the sulky and lift it up and flip the guy out of his bike.

Today, he most likely would get set down by the judges for these maneuvers.

Thomas also won three Hambletonians (all with fillies) and two Kentucky Futurities. Some of the great horses that

Thomas trained or drove were Dean Hanover, Cold Cash, McLin Hanover, Atlantic Hanover, Shirley Hanover, and Yankee Maid.

Thomas would claim three Hambletonian victories in eight years, and in 1934 he would claim three "heat world record" with the great pacer Cold Cash, which would stand for twenty-six years.

He always had a top stable and was considered a great horseman, having trained for the Hanover Shoe Farms stables.

Henry Thomas was also good friends with and trained horses for actor James Cagney.

Clint Hodgins

Clint Hodgins 6/18/07–1979

When Roosevelt Raceway first opened its doors in the forties, a man named Clinton Hodgins would become a contender for the driving honors nearly every single year.

He was consistent and aggressive, which made him a favorite among the bettors. The gamblers loved to bet him for they knew they would get their money's worth.

The list of great horses Hodgins steered to victory during his career was many. A few of them were Prince Adios, Proximity, Katie Key, and Elaine Rodney.

Two horses that Clint drove would one day become known as some of the best sires in the history of harness racing. They were Adios Butler and Bye Bye Byrd. In 1940,

Clint set a world record with a two-year-old trotting filly named Acrasia.

Although Clint was a pleasure to work for and sometimes a jokester, he was a serious businessman who made his employees walk a straight line. Every day he gave his grooms eight pebbles each and would instruct them to throw one at him each time they passed him while jogging a horse. This was his way of making sure each horse was exercised the proper distance.

Two of Hodgins' apprentices would turn out to be two of the greatest drivers in the history of harness racing—Buddy Gilmour and Lucien Fontaine. Hodgins taught his young students very well.

Later in his career, Clint would winter train in Orlando, Florida, and maintained a residence there until his death at the age of seventy-two.

A highlight in Hodgins career came on Nov. 24, 1939, when he won eleven races on a racing program at Dufferin Park.

Del Miller with Adios

Delvin Miller

Delvin Miller was known by many as "The Racing Giant" for his many victories in driving and training standardbreds. He was from the old school, and like O'Brien, he loved to see how close he could come to another driver while racing.

One of Miller's quirks was that he liked to chew glass to show people how macho he was. It was a habit that he picked up while in the US Calvary.

During his career he won 2,442 races and $11 million in purses.

Del, as he was called by his friends, was the sport's ambassador of good will and an innovator who helped promote it around the world. Miller is believed to be the only professional athlete to compete in nine decades. He was involved in every aspect of harness racing: first as a driver, then as a trainer, owner, and breeder.

Miller traveled the world to drive harness horses, stopping in Russia, New Zealand, Sweden, France, Germany, and said if there was racing in the Arctic, he would go there too!

Probably Del Miller is best known for once owning the Meadows Racetrack in Pennsylvania.

In 1948, Miller purchased a stallion named Adios. They made a winning team and won many races. After Adios's racing career was over, Miller stood him stud on his Meadowlands Farm. The horse proved to be a tremendous stud and was considered by many to be the greatest sire in the history of harness racing. Every year, the Meadows Racetrack has a race in honor of the horse called "The Adios."

Miller was friends with and trained horses for celebrities like Mickey Mantle, Whitey Ford, and Arnold Palmer. Miller died of heart failure at the age of eighty-three.

ॐ

The drivers mentioned above were just a handful of the many great drivers during the meets at Roosevelt Raceway.

There are many more drivers who deserve to be mentioned and honored, for each one, in their own special way, helped make Roosevelt Raceway the greatest track in the world and harness racing the wonderful sport it is today.

We hope to include your favorite.

(Note: It is not the author's intention to omit any driver in particular.)

Drivers Old timers night 1987 L-R George Phalen,
Jack Richardson, Frank Darish, Stanley Dancer, Jimmy
Cruise, Dick Thomas, Hugh MacIntosh and Del Miller

Other Legendary Drivers at Roosevelt

William "Billy" Hudson

Billy was a second-generation harness driver/trainer who
started racing at the age of seven at the fairs in Maryland.
After moving to New York in 1951, Hudson soon became
one of the most sought after "catch drivers" on the New
York circuit. Throughout his career, he amassed over $2
million for his owners. On October 13, 1963, a fire broke
out at Roosevelt Raceway in the stable area. Sadly, Hudson
lost fifteen of his twenty-one horses. During the fifties
and sixties, he was regarded as one of America's top catch

drivers. Billy's son, Freddie, would follow in his father's footsteps, training and driving horses, and is actively involved in the business today. (Note: Freddie is one of the authors of this book.)

Keith Waples

In Canada, they consider Keith Waples "the greatest horseman ever." As a young boy of twelve, Waples started driving harness horses at county fairs. His first winner was a horse named Grey Ghost, but the highlight in his career came in winning the Roosevelt International Trot with Tie Silk in 1962, and winning the Lady Maud at Roosevelt with Belle Acton in 1967.

Frank Ervin

Frank drove his first race at the age of sixteen, and won his first race that year by driving the trotter Black Diamond. Some of his other winning drives were with Sampson Hanover, Expression, Yankee Hanover, Bret Hanover, Impish, and Sprite Rodney. Ervin was also active in breeding and owned several broodmares. He also owned an interest in the champion racehorse called Good Time.

Billy Myer

Myer was one of the best catch drivers in his days. In a two-year span, Billy won ten "two minute miles," and won eight stake races, including the Battle of Saratoga, Cane Futurity, Commodore, Fox, Hanover-Hempt, Roosevelt Futurity, and the Shepherd.

George Phalen

Fans called him "Railing Phalen." At the age of six, George was jogging racehorses and drove his first race at the age of twelve. He bought a horse named Adios Butler, with his partner, a man named Paige West for $7,000. (Adios Butler would eventually go on to set a world record). George also set world records with horses Steamin Demon, Silver Song, and O'Brien Hanover. In his career, Phalen amassed over 1,500 wins and earnings of over $5,000,000.

Sacher "Satch" Warner

Warner's racing career spanned over a half century and two continents. Growing up in his native country of Austria, Warner was employed at a perfume company, but his heart was with the horses. He drove the horse Kairos in Europe, who was the sire of the 1960 Roosevelt International Trot hero, Hairos II.

Vernon Dancer

Brother to the renowned driver/trainer Stanley, Vernon followed in his brothers footsteps. He bought his first horse, Miss Norah, and won with her in 2:12. Miss Norah would become one of the best broodmares in the industry. She was the dam of Country Don, Uncle Duck, and Joan's Boy. Vernon was known for his patience and ability in developing great trotters.

Robert Cherrix

Although Cherrix had a moderately small stable, he was still considered a well-respected horseman. In 1959, when he first started to race at Roosevelt, he won seven of his first eight starts as a driver. In his first six years in the sport, his stable earned over $109,000. After twelve seasons, the figure climbed to over $1 million. Cherrix died at an early age due to cancer.

Ted Wing

Ted Wing was one of the most talented driver/trainers to hail from New England. Wing got into harness racing after having a successful career as an alpine ski champion. He amassed 5,199 wins and $32,905,784 in lifetime earnings.

Hugh Bell

In the 1950s and into the early 1960s, Hugh Bell was considered New York's "best catch driver." When the top stables in the country sent their horses to Roosevelt or Yonkers, they all sought out Bell's services to drive their horses.

Jimmy Jordan was one of Roosevelt Raceway's early leading drivers, winning the title in 1942. In the 1930s through the 1950s, Jordan was one of the nation's top drivers. He was a very soft spoken man who was nicknamed harness racing's "Mr. Nice Guy." Jimmy Jordan's first Roosevelt Raceway drive was on September 3, 1940, which was the track's second night of racing.

Leading Drivers at Roosevelt Raceway
from 1940 to 1986

Year	Driver	Starts	Wins	Seconds	Thirds	
UDRS						
1940	Carl Dill	N/A	N/A	N/A	N/A	.385
1941	Minter Dennison	N/A	N/A	N/A	N/A	.489
1942	James Jordan	N/A	N/A	N/A	N/A	.611
1943	Record Unavailable					
1944	Clint Hodgins	N/A	N/A	N/A	N/A	.872
1945	Frank Safford	N/A	N/A	N/A	N/A	.934
1946	Frank Safford	N/A	N/A	N/A	N/A	.1061
1947	Frank Safford	N/A	N/A	N/A	N/A	.1239
1948	Henry Thomas	193	37	31	23	.350
1949	Wayne Smart	130	34	20	14	.383
1950	John Simpson, Sr.	213	57	35	36	.415
1951	Henry Thomas	143	32	24	19	.361
1952	John Simpson Sr.	159	36	28	27	.381
1953	Hugh Bell	87	20	15	14	.379
1954	Richard Thomas	143	30	17	26	.336
1955	Stanley Dancer	363	81	58	59	.356
1956	Robert Walker	94	25	12	9	.358
1957	William Haughton	266	49	53	37	.342
1958	Jimmy Cruise	214	43	41	19	.337
1959	Stanley Dancer	162	31	27	18	.356
1960	Stanley Dancer	251	60	46	29	.380
1961	Stanley Dancer	153	31	28	19	.346
1962	Stanley Dancer	162	45	24	21	.403
1963	George Sholty	305	69	51	49	.374
1964	Stanley Dancer	183	51	22	20	.382
1965	William Haughton	334	79	55	45	.387
1966	Del Insko	761	141	101	90	.300
1967	George Sholty	542	103	84	50	.325
1968	Carmine Abbatiello	638	129	109	87	.344
1969	George Sholty	308	72	47	40	.362
1970	Carmine Abbatiello	729	145	111	94	.327
1971	Herve Filion	450	98	66	63	.347
1972	Herve Filion	761	144	116	94	.315
1973	Herve Filion	707	116	133	104	.318
1974	Herve Filion	904	187	161	116	.349

1975	Buddy Gilmour	732	150	116	93	.335
1976	Carmine Abbatiello	569	115	89	62	.325
1977	Carmine Abbatiello	824	174	120	111	.337
1978	Carmine Abbatiello	832	180	132	96	.343
1979	Carmine Abbatiello	925	187	133	110	.322
1980	William O'Donnell	193	38	32	29	.339
1981	Carmine Abbatiello	759	157	119	89	.333
1982	William O'Donnell	283	45	48	41	.302
1983	Carmine Abbatiello	817	161	122	106	.323
1984	Mike LaChance	1165	224	177	152	.320
1985	Mike LaChance	1383	302	220	179	.350
1986	Leo Bauer	415	77	88	104	.387

Other Great Drivers of Roosevelt Raceway

Tony Abbatiello...Frank Albertson...Vinny
Aurigemma...Earl Avery...Paul Appel...Frank
Annunziato...Alan Alkes...Howard Beissinger...Ralph
Baldwin...George Butterworth...Joe Bonacorsa...
Kevin Bonacorsa...Don Bonacorsa...John Barchi...
Larry Battaglia...Al Burton...George Berkner...Lee
Benson...Jerry Bostic...Dick Baker...Fred Bradbury...
Eddie Cobb...Real (Coco) Cormier...Henry Clukey...
Cecil Champion...Mike Crocco...Herman Carbone...
Jim Crane...Bobby Camper...Jim Curran...Peter
Cashman...Del Cameron...Jimmy Cruise, Jr.,...Earl
Cruise...John Campbell...Howard Camden...Dick
Custis...Harold (Sonny) Dancer, Jr.,...Jim Dennis...
Bill Dennis...Ted Dennis...Alfred "Bucky" Day...Benny
Defonce...Jacques Dupuis...Norman Dauplaise...Jeff
Dauplaise...Merrit (Butch) Dokey...Rejean Daigneault...
Wendy Daigneault...Mike Dolan...Luca Derrico...Frank
Darish...John Darish...Don Darish...Donnie Dancer...
Ronnie Dancer...Harold Dancer, Sr.,...Jean Drolet...
Jim Doherty...Dave Dunkley...Carl Dill...John Dill...

Minter (Whitey) Dennison...John Edmunds...Tom
Foster...Joe Faraldo...Bobby Frame...Henri Filion...
Mike Forte...Charles Fitzpatrick...Joe Firetti...Tom
(Red) Faulhaber...Marc Fontaine...Will Fleming...Vic
Fleming...Charlie Fleming...Mike Gagliardi...Marc
Gilmour...Joe Grasso...Franki Galante...Mike Galante...
Jim Grundy...Peter Haughton...Tommy Haughton...
Cammie Haughton...Bobby Hiel...Roger Hammer...
John (Red) Hanafin...Freddie Hudson...Levi Harner...
Eldon Harner...Harry Harvey...Eddie Hart...Evert
Hope...Austin Hope...Pat Iovine...Joel Jason...John
Kopas...Jack Kopas...Arthur Koch...Mike Lachance...
Sandy Levy...Skip Lewis...Eddie Lohmeyer...Mike Lizzi
Sr.,...Mike Lizzi, Jr.,...John LaBarge...Jimmy Marohn...
Bill (Footsie) Mitchell...Mickey McNichol...Kenny
McNutt...Archie McNeil...Frank Mule...Alan Myer...
Paul Myer...Eddie Myer...Gary Myer...Lou Miller...
Frank Mollica...Lou Meittinis...Jim (Par Four) Marcus...
John Miritello...Gene MacDonald...Joe MacDonald...
Gene Mattucci...Hugh MacIntosh...Tom Merriman...
Joe Marsh, Jr.,...Cat Manzi...Gerald MacDonald...
Morrie MacDonald...Winky Mello...Archie Niles,
Jr...Buck Norris...Scot Norris...Bruce Nickells...Arlo
Nelson...Bill O'Donnell...William Popfinger...Frank
Popfinger...Henry Pownall..John (Sonny) Patterson,
Jr.,...John Patterson, Sr.,...Jerry Procino...Maurice
Pusey...Jim Phalen...Les Pullen...John Paton...Randy
Perry...Jack Quinn...Nat Ray...Joe Ricco...Sanders
Russell...Bobby Rahner...Ray Remmen...Buddy
Regan...Jack Richardson...Jim Rankin...Mike Santa
Maria...Bobby Shuttleworth...Donny Sider...Benny
Steall...Jerry Sarama...Bobby Scores.. Larry Summers...

Mel Smorra...Sam Smith...John Simpson, Jr.,...Tom Santeramo.. Jay Tremblay...Frank Tagariello...Jimmy Tallman...Eldon Turcotte...Mel Turcotte...Al (Apples) Thomas...Dave Tovin...Linda Toscano...Andy Toscano... Rocky Toscano...Dover Tolson...Dick Thomas...Ben Turlington...Larry VanOstrand...Bobby VanOstrand... Bobby Vitrano...Gilles Villemure...Paul Vineyard... Paige West...Bobby Walker...Tommy Winn... Tommy Wingate...George Wampetich...Wendell Wathen, Jr.,...Walt Warrington and Eddie Wheeler.

2

Stories Remembered

Throughout the many glorious years that Roosevelt Raceway was operating, many events and situations took place that became "legends" to many people. Most of them are funny, some are hard to believe—but believe us, they really did happen! In this section, we have listed as many as space would allow. We hope you enjoy them as much as we did!

The Runaway Bike

It was during the time that horsemen were switching over from the conventional sulky to the modified sulky. A driver/trainer named Russell Rash began making his own version in his garage. He gave one of the homemade sulkies to trainer Freddie Hudson. One day when Freddie was getting ready to go a training mile on the main track at Roosevelt, he noticed that the bike didn't feel just right. As he passed other drivers on the track, they were asking him what was wrong with his bike. Suddenly Freddie noticed his seat was getting lower to the ground and the wheels on the bike were pointing outward. Immediately, Hudson got off of the bike and walked his horse back to the stable area, where everyone was laughing. The next day, they returned the newly made sulky back to its maker, Rash, and got a full refund. That was the end of Russell Rash's career of making race bikes.

Archie Niles, Jr. "The Pool Shark"

One day at Roosevelt Raceway, they announced over the PA system that they were looking for a driver who was good at playing pool (billiards) to participate in an exhibition game with Willie Mosconi. The horseman all agreed Archie Niles Jr. was the harness drivers' best pool player. So as not to be too embarrassed, Archie practiced eight hours a day for the next two weeks before the exhibition. When the time came for the exhibition, Niles was as good as he could be. Niles ran the table on Mosconi three times until the management had to stop him from shooting so his opponent could shoot.

Super Louie Saves the Day—
And a Marriage

A man named Michael "Smash" Urgo, who lived in Albany, New York, was good friends with driver Bobby "Bullet" Vitrano. That evening, Vitrano was driving three horses at Roosevelt Raceway. Urgo drove to the track and found Vitrano in the track kitchen sitting at a table talking to a group of people. When Bobby saw Urgo, he got up from the table and went over to see his friend. Vitrano told his friend that he liked the horse named Super Louie the best of his three drives, but the horse had post position 8. Vitrano said for Urgo to stand by the fence when Bobby scores his horse down and he would nod if the horse looked good. When Vitrano scored the horse down, he nodded his head, telling Urgo he liked the way the horse warmed up. As Urgo went to the window to bet the horse, a Jamaican man walked up to him and told him he lost his pay check and noticed Vitrano nodding to Michael. The distraught man said he only had $20 in his pocket and would like to make some money betting, if possible. Urgo told the man to bet number 8, as he did shortly after. When Urgo went to the bar to find his wife, the bartender asked him who he bet. When Urgo told him, the bartender replied, "That horse doesn't have a shot." Feeling good about his bet, Urgo told the bartender that if the horse didn't finish first or second, Urgo would buy drinks for everyone at the bar—but if Vitrano finished first or second, the bartender had to buy the drinks for everyone. The race went off and Vitrano bolted out of the gate, went right to the top, and won the race handily. Embarrassed, the disgruntled bartender had to buy drinks for everyone at the bar. The horse Super Louie paid $58.00 to win! Urgo cashed $3,500 that race, having bet the horse to win, hit the Exacta and triple. As Urgo walked away from the window counting his money, the Jamaican man saw him, ran up to him, and laid a big one right on his lips. The grateful man thanked Urgo for the tip, saying that he saved his life from his wife!

The Wrong Becky

One afternoon, when trainer Howard "Buck" Norris was at home taking a nap, the phone rang. When he answered it, a woman on the other end asked him, "How's Becky doing?"

Thinking it was one of his owners inquiring about their horse, Becky Bell, Norris said, "I trained her this morning around twenty. She got a little lazy on me so I gave her a few shots with the whip, and she straightened out." The phone call happened to be from the school where his daughter attended, asking how she was doing, for she had been home that day sick.

A Sure Bet

One evening when trainer Freddie Hudson only had one or two horses in to drive at Roosevelt Raceway, he made a pit stop at the Gam Wah. The owner of Gam Wah, a man named Harry Mock, asked Hudson to walk to the track with him. As they were walking through the grandstand, Mock asked Hudson who he liked in the upcoming race. Ironically, there was a horse in that race that Hudson had trained alongside with that week, and the horse looked really good. So Hudson told Mock. In a split of a second, Mock flew to the windows to make a bet. Yes, the horse won!

Hey, You're Wearing My Colors!

One year, trainer/driver Billy Myer had a set of colors stolen from the locker room at Roosevelt Raceway. About a month later, as Myer was driving down Post Avenue, he spotted a kid walking down the street wearing his stolen colors. Immediately, Myer pulls his car over and yells to the thief to stop and that he was wearing his colors. Immediately, the young man took off running in Myer's colors, but the trainer was unable to catch him. He never did get his colors back!

An Affair to Remember

One night at Roosevelt Raceway, a race mare named Misty Flight escaped from her stall, and, unknowingly to anyone, had "an affair to remember." A little shy of a year later, on May 13, 1962 (Mothers' Day), Misty Flight gave birth to a colt who was named Roosevelt Baby. He was a late foal and on the small size, so he was not raced as a two-year-old. As a three-year-old, Roosevelt Baby raced three times at Rockingham Park. They were all nonbetting races. On May 23, 1965, the colt made his racing debut at Roosevelt Raceway. With driver Johnny Chapman in the sulky, Roosevelt Baby broke stride in the first turn and made up many lengths, coming four wide through the stretch and finishing third, missing second by a nose. When Chapman was being interviewed after the race, he was quoted as saying, "The two recalls and the lights excited Roosevelt Baby at the start, causing him to go off stride, but he trotted wonderfully in the end." Any movie deal based on this one night fling, went up in smoke.

Hit and Run

One day, driver Jimmy Cruise read in the newspaper that a man who was driving on Old Country Road had been in an accident. He blamed it on the fact that a goat ran in front of his car. Jimmy realized that a goat was missing from his stable the evening in question, decided to hide the goat so he could not be sued if they blamed his goat. Cruise brought his goat over to the barn of his friend, Billy Hudson, where it remained for several months. After several months passed and Cruise was never questioned, the goat returned home to the Cruise stable.

Give Me Your Wallet

Once there was a man who was going around robbing people at gunpoint in the parking lots of local restaurants. A man named Cal Coolidge, the stable superintendant, told his friends that nobody was ever going to rob him—that he would fight them to his death if they tried to rob him. About three weeks later, as he pulled into one of the parking lots and was getting out of his car, a man jumped him and said, "Give me your wallet!"

Not only did brave Cal give the robber his wallet, but he said, "Wait a minute. I have more money in this pocket!" and handed him his money.

What Color Wig Do You Want?

"Harry the Wig" was a horse owner who had horses with Billy Haughton. Harry Levinson owned factories around the world that made over two million different wigs per year. Harry came up with the brilliant idea of making wigs for racehorses to wear on their tails and manes in the racing colors of either the trainers or owners. He presented the idea to Roosevelt Raceway who decided to use the wigs in the 1966 International Trot. While they were testing the idea, the wigs would not stay on the horses' tails, so they decided to try using them on their manes. George Morton Levy and Roosevelt Raceway made wigs in every country's colors, and the horses wore them during the post parade in the International Trot. Of course the wigs were removed before the horses raced.

Waiting on the Rest of the Field

It was a foggy night at the races. The visibility was very poor—the drivers could only see a short distance ahead. Out of the gate, driver Alan Myer took his horse to the front and raced him on the outside in order to get better visibility. Once on top, he slowed the horse down and waited to hear the other horses coming. Although his horse wanted to go, Alan had him under wraps. On the top of the stretch heading for home, Myer put his horse into gear and drew off, ahead of the field, winning the race by ten lengths. The funny thing is that Myer really only raced his horse for half a mile, although nobody noticed.

Will the Real Frank Popfinger Please Stand Up?

One night before the races, a man walks into Mimmo's, walks up to the bar, and orders a drink. Sitting at the bar were driver/trainers Jack Richardson and Archie Niles Jr. After the man finishes his drink, he orders another. He soon starts a conversation with Richardson and Niles, introducing himself as Frank Popfinger. Unbeknownst to the man, the two drivers were good friends with the real Popfinger, and they let him rattle on. The man claiming to be Frank Popfinger tells his new two "friends" that he has three horses in races that evening, and not to bet him for he would be "stiffing" all of them. Finally, one of the drivers said to the phony that Frank Popfinger was a good friend of his, and that the imposter was *not* who he said he was. Embarrassed and in shock, the man excused himself to go the restroom…and never returned!

A Good Tip

One day, trainer/driver Billy Hudson went to the barber shop to get a haircut. The barber gave Hudson a "tip" on a horse that ironically, Hudson was scheduled to drive. When Billy asked him who he got the tip from, the barber said, "I got it from Billy Hudson, the driver. He was in here yesterday to get a haircut!

Jamin winning 1959 International

Jamin in winners circle 1959 International Trot

3

The Track Announcer

Jack E. Lee

Jack E. Lee

When we took a poll and asked people who their favorite racetrack announcer was, many said it was a man named Jack E. Lee. Lee was the track announcer at Roosevelt Raceway back in the early seventies. His mellifluous baritone resonated throughout the track, even being heard over all the moans, groans, and excitement of the patrons.

It is not an easy job being a racetrack announcer, for they have to memorize each horse and driver in every race. This is usually around eighty different horses per racing night. And on top of that, the announcer has to make each and every race sound as exciting as if it was the Hambletonian. Not an easy task at all. Track announcers at half-mile tracks can easily get locked into a formula. The races all unfold in similar fashion, and are run mostly all at the same distance—featuring the leader, the unfortunate first one over, the horse getting the pocket trip (sitting behind the leading horse), fourth with perfect cover on the outside, and the dreaded third on the rail (this holds true especially in the days before the passing lane.)

The late great Jack E. Lee avoided slipping into monotony with the sheer power and grace of his voice, and an unfailing accuracy which made the visuals virtually unnecessary. Lee's deep, smooth voice was known to millions in the New York City area where he was track announcer at Roosevelt Raceway during the track's late glory years from 1968 to 1985.

Lee was also public address announcer for The New York Mets and Madison Square Garden, where he was ring announcer for World Wrestling Federation shows.

Harness Racing lost one of the best track announcers in the history of harness racing when Jack E. Lee died of a heart attack on July 30, 2009. "Jack, you gave us the ultimate thrill in hearing each and every race you called. We will never forget you. Hope you are calling the races up above for all to enjoy!" RIP.

Clem McCarthy

When it first opened its doors in the forties, the first announcer at Roosevelt Raceway was a man who, at the time, was the most famous sportscaster—Clem McCarthy.

Clem was born in Rochester, New York, and was one of the most famous race track and public address announcers. He was known for his gravelly voice and dramatic style—a "whiskey tenor." Clem was also the first public announcer at a major American racetrack, Arlington Park in Arlington Heights, Illinois. In addition to being a race caller for racetracks and NBC Radio, he was a top boxing announcer as well.

He is probably best remembered as the race announcer who called the famous Seabiscuit/War Admiral match race, including this phrase in the final stretch run as Seabiscuit shocked the horse racing world by outrunning the heavily favored War Admiral: "Seabiscuit by three! Seabiscuit by three!"

Jerry Glantz

After Jack E. Lee stepped down from the duty as race track announcer at Roosevelt Raceway, he was replaced by a man named Jerry Glantz.

Jerry started his career at Monticello Racetrack and spent many years after that at Pompano Racetrack. When the opportunity arose to go to Roosevelt, Jerry made the move. He quickly became popular with the fans and horsemen, considering being what some said was "a hard act to follow," especially, in Jack E. Lee's footsteps. But Glantz proved himself as one of the best.

Glantz continued calling the races at Roosevelt Raceway and it was his voice that was heard calling the horses as they came to the finish line on that fateful day of July 15, 1988 (the final racing day at Roosevelt Raceway).

𝕊ℂ

As you can see, there are people behind the scenes who are involved in the racing of horses that are equally as important as the person who sits behind the horse. The adrenalin rush we get and the thrill when hearing the track announcer call the race, up until his very last word as the winning horse crosses the finish line, is exhilarating and priceless.

4

The International Trot

**By: Barry Lefkowitz—Roosevelt Raceway's
Publicity Director**

The publicity department and press box at Roosevelt
Raceway was certainly the busiest for events such
as the International Trot and the Messenger
Stakes. During my years as Publicity Director, the
department consisted of myself as Director, Mike
Cohen as Assistant Director, Lew Barasch as
Director of Special Events and Kay Cisco as our
assistant and secretary.

Lou Miller, the former sportswriter and horse
trainer was on hand to add valuable assistance in
writing press releases. Although she wasn't on staff,
Grace "Bunny" Barasch, Lew's charming wife,
would help invaluably during the International
festivities.

The International Trot was, of course, the
highlight of our season. From the minute the race
days were approved by the State and the date of

the International was secured, it was full steam ahead for those three weeks in July or August that included the American Trotting Championship, International and Challenge Cup. It was the publicity department's responsibility to help select the horses to compete, make sure the travel arrangements were made, hosting all of the connections for two weeks and to promote the event.

As can be imagined, the International series requires lots of planning and lots of special approvals. This included waivers from national and local agencies. The International and Challenge Cup were considered as one event for tax purposes. The track had to get special permission to eliminate the normal quarantine barn and closing the track at specific intervals during the day to allow the foreign horses to get accustomed to the track.

From the very beginning of the year, we would be keeping a sharp eye on the foreign trotting scene, beginning in January with the Prix d' Amerique in Paris and the Elitlop in Sweden, looking for the top horses to invite.

As the race would get closer, we would decide which foreign horses to invite and place under contract. As the race drew closer we would start talking to all the various media outlets, gain interest about the race and look for the people in charge to assign their staffers to cover the event.

At the same time, we would decide where we would hold the post-position draw press conference and the International Gala, which was held at different places such as Old Westbury Gardens on the Thursday evening before the race.

The foreign horses would start coming in a bit before the American Trotting Championship, the race to decide the two horses to represent the U.S. in the series. From then on, until the last horse left to head back home, it was non-stop, 24 hours a day. During week before the International, we would be working tirelessly coming up with story ideas for the various reporters, being careful not to give the same angle to more than one person.

The night of the race was so intense. I felt like I needed roller skates, I must have walked through the entire plant 30 times during the night. The main concern was making sure all of the details were taken care of. This was accomplished with tremendous co-ordination and co-operation from all of the track's departments and staff.

And let us not forget all the other people that enabled us to pull it off. For example, we had to make sure we had interpreters lined up for every language needed. But it was up to the publicity department to pull it off, for there could not be any mistakes. Each department had to put on extra staffing for the event— it was all hands on deck. The smallest detail could not be overlooked, such as making sure the elevator leading to the press box being held on the ground floor after the race, ensuring no time was wasted.

The International, like all major sporting events was covered by an overflow of media members and we had to make sure each one had what they needed to do their job. This normally included large contingent of foreign press.

The evening started off with a cocktail party reception for the media members and their spouses. Then off to the Cloud Casino for dinner. As the race drew closer, the press moved to the press box to start their job. The press box, needless to say, was packed beyond capacity. All of the major daily newspapers, industry trade publications and foreign press were represented.

After the race and winner's circle presentation concluded, now the race for the publicity department was on! Since the race was held later in the evening, we were under real deadlines to get the story out. A security detail escorted the winning trainer, driver and connections, to the elevator leading to the press box. After the post-race interviews, everyone was busy writing their stories, then jockeying phones around to meet their deadlines. We had a currier waiting for video of the race to drive them around New York City to the TV stations. With the race over and the stories out, it was time to relax and sit down for a minute.

But the rest was short lived. The next morning we were up early, getting barn photo opportunities and then it was another busy week hosting all of the participants leading up to the Challenge Cup. We were all exhausted after the event but none of us would trade it for anything.

80CR

Below is a list stating the year, which horse was victorious, the country they represented, the time the race was won, and the purse amount for the race. As you can see, the purse increased as the years went by.

Roosevelt International Trot Winners

Year	Winner	Driver	Country	Time	Purse
1959	Jamin	Riaud	France	3:08.3	$50,000
(note: distance 1 ½ miles)					
1960	Hairos II	Geersen	Netherlands	2:34	$50,000
1961	Su Mac Lad	Dancer	United States	2:34.2	$50,000
1962	Tie Silk	Waples	Canada	2:34.1	$50,000
1963	Su Mac Lad	Dancer	United States	2:32.3	$50,000
1964	Speedy Scot	Baldwin	United States	2:32.3	$50,000
1965	Pluvier III	Nordin	Sweden	2:36.2	$100,000
1966	Armbro Flight	O'Brien	United States	2:31.3	$100,000
1967	Roquepine	Levesque	France	2:43.4	$100,000
1968	Roquepine	Gougeon	France	2:38.3	$100,000
1969	Une de Mai	Gougeon	France	2:33.2	$100,000
1970	Fresh Yankee	O'Brien	Canada	2:35.1	$125,000
1971	Une de Mai	Gougeon	France	2:34.4	$125,000
1972	Speedy Crown	Beissinger	United States	2:35.1	$125,000
1973	Delmonica Hanover	Chapman	United States	2:34.2	$150,000
1974	Delmonica Hanover	Chapman	United States	2:34.4	$200,000
1975	Savoir	Insko	United States	2:32.1	$200,000
1976	Equileo	Froger	France	2:33.3	$200,000
1977	Delfo	Brighenti	Italy	2:34.3	$200,000
1978	Cold Comfort	Haughton	United States	2:31.1	$200,000
1979	Doublemint	Haughton	United States	2:38.	$200,000
1980	Classical Way	Simpson Jr.	United States	2:35.2	$250,000
1981	Ideal du Gazeau	Lefevre	France	2:32.3	$250,000
1982	Ideal du Gazeau	Lefevre	France	2:36	$250,000
1983	Idealdu Gazeau	Lefevre	France	2:35.1	$250,000
1984	Lutin d'Isigny	Andre	France	2:30	$250,000**
1985	Lutin d'Isigny	Andre	France	2:30	$250,000
1986	Habib	Thorsen	Norway	2:33	$250,000
1987	Callit	Karl Johansson	Sweden	2:33.4	$200,000

** World record

Although it has been years since the International Trot took place at Roosevelt Raceway, the history and records that were set there during that time will live on forever. The fabulous equine athletes that participated in these races deserve praise and admiration for the hard work and great performances they did to entertain the public. The International Trot was last raced in 1987 at Roosevelt Raceway. From there it had moved to other various tracks.

"Thanks for the memories."

5

The Famous Horses
of Roosevelt Raceway

"Never send a man to do a horse's job."

—Mr. Ed

There's no doubt that Roosevelt Raceway was one of the best harness tracks in history, but it wasn't just the ambiance or the glitz that made it so exciting, or the high-profile trainers and drivers that called Roosevelt their home. Probably one of the most important and compelling things that made Roosevelt a legend were the outstanding horses that competed there, continuously setting new track and world records. People would go there just to watch their favorite horse entertain them by giving a thrilling and nail-biting stretch drive race to the end.

There were thousands of horses— trotters and pacers, fillies and mares, and colts, geldings and stallions that helped make Roosevelt the legendary "Dream Track" it was. When we asked people who their favorite standardbred horse was, we received hundreds of different answers. Some of the horses were renowned, others were crowd favorites, and some were horses they personally owned. Regardless of who your favorite horse was, there, undoubtedly, are thousands that should be mentioned and honored. Each and every one of the horses who, at one time or another, had their hooves over the famous RR surface did it for the entertainment of the people and to make their owners, trainers, fans, and grooms proud.

The top horses in both categories (pacers and trotters) were track- or world-record holders, or in some way were legends in their own right.

Legendary Trotters

The Famous Horses
Su Mac Lad

Su Mac Lad (Potomac Lad—Spuds Sue) 1:58.4

$885,095

During "the golden years" at Roosevelt Raceway, a horse named Su Mac Lad was known as harness racing's "golden gelding."

He was owned by I. W. Berkemeyer and trained and driven by Stanley Dancer. On September 28, 1962, he set a new track record of 2:00 flat. At that time, he was the world's leading money winning trotter, racing against the top horses across the country.

Su Mac Lad had a history of getting painful quarter crack injuries. The gelding had the misfortune of developing this problem at least six times throughout his racing career, which deterred his racing schedule.

He won the International Trot at Roosevelt Raceway in both 1961(the first American trotter to do so) and 1963, and was voted "Trotter of the Year" in both of those years. As a two-year-old, the trotter was sold for $750 and, in 1959, Mr. Berkemeyer bought the gelding for $35,000.

The beautiful gelding died at the age of twenty-eight at Stanley Dancer's farm, where he lived following his retirement from racing.

Richard Stone Reeves picture of Delmonica Hanover

Delmonica Hanover (Speedy Count—Delicious)

John Chapman was the proud trainer/owner of the mare Delmonica Hanover. Delmonica was a beautiful trotting mare who was voted "Horse of the Year" in 1974.

She was a fearless competitor who did not get intimidated by racing against the top males.

Delmonica was the chief rival of world champion Super Bowl many times throughout her career. Although she was up against colts, she finished second in both heats of the Hambletonian, and trotted what would have been world filly marks.

The gorgeous mare won the International Trot at Roosevelt Raceway on two occasions–1973 and 1974– which caught the attention of the industries, top prospective buyers and breeders. In 1974, Delmonica won the prestigious Prix D'Amerique at Vincennes Racetrack in Paris, France.

Speedy Scot

Speedy Scot (Speedster—Scotch Love) 3, 1:56.4

$650,909

Speedy Scot was foaled in 1960 at Castleton Farm in Kentucky. He was sired by Speedster and his dam was Scotch Love. He earned his place in the standardbred history books by setting world records and siring top performers.

In 1962, as a two-year-old, he won fourteen of nineteen starts, and trotted to a mark of 2:01.1—a very respectable time for a juvenile trotting colt. The next year, as a three-year-old, he stormed to the pinnacle of the sport by becoming the second horse to capture the trotting triple crown.

At four, he continued to maintain his championship form, defeating such free-for-all stars such as Su Mac Lad and Duke Rodney. The thirty-year-old stallion died peacefully in 1990 at Castleton Farms, where he had lived for all but the three years he spent at racetracks.

Nevele Pride

Nevele Pride (Stars Pride—Thankful) 1:54.4

$871,738

Nevele Pride was driven and trained by Stanley Dancer. Throughout his racing career Nevele won fifty-seven races and was voted the "Harness Horse of the Year" for three consecutive years.

When he was a yearling, Dancer spotted the horse on a farm. He loved his looks and paid $20,000 for him. He then sold part of the horse to Louis Resnick and Nevele Acres.

Nevele was a junk food lover who loved hot dogs and cigarettes. (He ate them, he didn't smoke them)

He won many races, including the Hambletonian, the Yonkers Futurity, both heats of the Kentucky Futurity, the Triple Crown of Harness Racing, and the Realization Trot at Roosevelt Raceway.

Using three thoroughbred horses, known in the industry as "prompters," to maintain his speed, Nevele Pride broke the world record" at the Indiana State Fairgrounds, covering a mile in the time of 1:54 4/5. This was done in front of twelve thousand people. The three prompters were driven by Billy Haughton, Vernon Dancer, and Delvin Miller.

The horse earned more than $870,000 during his racing career. This phenomenal feat broke the record that was held by Greyhound, since the 1930's.

Nevele Pride hung up his harness when he retired in a ceremony on October 17, 1969. After his retirement, Nevele Pride was shipped to Stoner Creek Stud in Paris, Kentucky. He proved to be as good a stud as he was a racehorse.

The handsome stud died on February 19, 1993, in Lexington, Kentucky.He was laid to rest alongside the great pacing sire Meadow Skipper and the thoroughbred champion, Count Fleet.

Une de Mai

Une de Mai (Really Noble—Viens Danser)

Une de Mai was a copper-colored French mare who made the stallions racing against her work for their money. Une de Mai was one of the best trotting mares in the history of harness racing and was a world-record holder.

She was foaled in France and was driven by Jean-Rene Gougeon, known in France as "Le Pape" (because supposedly he resembled Pope Paul).

Going into the International Trot, the incredible Une de Mai already amassed earnings of $1,238,355—a world record at that time for a harness horse. Une de Mai also won the International Trot in 1969 and 1971.

When Une de Mai retired from racing, Roosevelt Raceway had a retirement ceremony in the winner's circle, and as in the racing tradition, her shoes were pulled in public—as a symbol of her retirement.

Elaine Rodney

Elaine Rodney (Rodney—Honor Bright)

1:58.3

Elaine Rodney was a hardworking race mare who was trained and driven by the legendary Clint Hodgins. She was called "the world's toughest trotting mare" by many.

As a two-year-old, she raced twenty-four times, and finished first sixteen and second five times. In 1960, she won the Kentucky Futurity in the fastest mile ever by a sophomore. Shortly after her win in the Futurity, Elaine Rodney was sold to the Italians, where she continued racing.

After her racing career was over, she became a top broodmare in Italy and the United States.

Duke Rodney

Duke "The Duke" Rodney (Rodney—Duke's Dutchess) 1:59

$639,408

Duke Rodney was trained and driven by Bill Haughton. Although the horse was small in stature, he compensated with his huge heart. He was a gutsy campaigner who loved to race. The Duke was bought at the Lexington Sale in 1959 for $7,000. As a three-year-old, the Duke trotted the fastest early season mile ever raced by a three-year-old on a half-mile track.

He was a world champion trotter in the late fifties and early sixties, and he was occasionally driven by Eddie Wheeler.

Duke Rodney was the greatest money-winning trotting stallion of his time.

Dream of Glory

Dream of Glory (Speedy Count—Dixie Valley)

At age two, Dream of Glory won fifteen out of nineteen starts, including the Ohio State Standardbred Futurity, Arden Downs, and five Ohio State Stakes. In his freshman year, Dream of Glory was driven by Mel Turcotte.

As a three-year-old and four-year-old, Dream of Glory was driven by Pius Soehnlen, and, then by Joe O'Brien at age five. He was the "USTA Champion" at ages three, four, and five and World Champion at age five.

Purchased in 1976 as a five-year-old by Armstrong Brothers and its partner Enterprise Stables, he joined the stallion ranks at Armstrong's Nursery in Inglewood, Ontario.

Dream of Glory retired as the all-age world record holder of the fastest mile (1:57.3) over a five-eighths-mile track, with fifty wins and twenty-four more "in the money" finishes in eighty-four starts.

As a stud, he sired winners of $47.9 million. He died at age twenty-one.

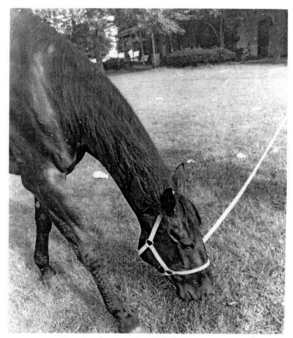

Fresh Yankee

Fresh Yankee (Hickory Pride—Pert Yankee)

$1.9 million

The life of the trotting mare Fresh Yankee is truly a Cinderella story: A "rags to riches" real life fairytale. In 1964, a man named Duncan MacDonald from Sydney, Nova Scotia, went to a yearling sale in Harrisburg to purchase a hobby horse to play around with on his farm. The mare was by far the best $900 investment Duncan MacDonald ever made.

The young horse was consigned to the sale by former New York Yankee outfielder Charley Keller. When MacDonald found out it would cost more to ship the filly to his country than what she cost him, he turned her over to horseman Sanders Russell to train.

After Sanders developed Fresh Yankee, he bowed out after her three-year-old campaign. Sanders thought that at age sixty-nine, he would be unable to face the exhausting pace that was ahead for the upcoming star.

MacDonald moved his prize mare over to Joe O'Brien, who developed a special rapport with her and played a huge part as she became the first North American-bred trotter to win $1 million.

The summary of her eight-year career was 89 wins, 44 seconds, and 24 thirds in 191 starts for $1.2 million, while setting or equaling five world records against the best trotters (male or female) in the world.

Fresh Yankee's awards and accomplishments would fill a page (or two).

She won the Roosevelt International Trot in 1970 and represented Canada six times.

Fresh Yankee retired as the second richest money-winning trotter in the world and died in 1991 at the age of twenty-eight.

Legendary Pacers

Niatross

Niatross (Albatross—Niagara Dream) 1:49.1

$2,021,213

Niatross was an American champion racehorse who many believe was the greatest harness horse of all time. He was trained and driven by co-owner Clint Galbraith.

The champion stallion was unbeaten in thirteen starts in his two-year-old season when he was named "Harness Horse of the Year."

After winning his first six lifetime starts, half-interest in the horse was sold to Lou Guida and the Niatross Syndicate for $2.5 million in cash.

In 1980, Niatross won the Meadowlands Pace which was the first million-dollar race in either standardbred or thoroughbred racing history. Niatross also won the Triple Crown of Harness Racing for Pacers.

During his racing career, Niatross won thirty-seven of thirty-nine races. By the time the horse retired to stud at Castleton Farm in 1981, he had earned more than any other standarbred horse in history.

In 1996, when Niatross was nineteen years old, he made a twenty-city tour for his beloved fans in the United States and Canada.

Niatross died at the age of twenty-two after being humanely euthanized due to a large cancerous mass in his abdomen.

Bye Bye Byrd

Bye Bye Byrd aka/"Mr. Everything" (Poplar Byrd—Evalina Hanover) 1:56.1

$554,257

At one time, a standardbred horse called Bye Bye Byrd was known as harness racing's "Mr. Everything."

Bye Bye Byrd was the good-looking big, stouthearted son of Poplar Byrd/Evalina Hanover. He set a track and world record on August 28, 1959.

After a sensational three-year-old season, the handsome pacer dominated the Metropolitan area for his trainer/driver, Clint Hodgins.

In addition to winning many Free-For-All and Fast Class events, Bye Bye Byrd won the $50,000 National Pacing Derby in the years 1959 and 1960.

When he retired to stud duty in 1961, Bye Bye Byrd was the leading money-winning harness horse with $554,257 in earnings.

Bye Bye Byrd passed away in 1980 at Hempt Farms in Pennsylvania at the age of twenty-five.

Bret Hanover

Bret Hanover (Hal Dale—Brennie Hanover) TT 1:53.3

$922,616

Bret Hanover was the first standarbred to be voted Horse of the Year three times, and he's the only horse that ever received that honor *up through today.*

Bret Hanover was trained and driven by Frank Ervin. He was undefeated as a two-year-old and voted Horse of the Year in 1964, 1965, and 1966. Bret Hanover was an extremely intelligent horse who loved to entertain his fans. After every win, Ervin would bring his "star" horse back in front of the crowd and get out of the sulky. Spontaneously, Bret would cross his front legs and bend over and bow before the crowd. What a showman (horse) and a ham!

Because of his unique style and fame, there have been many books written about him, including *Big Bum, The Story of Bret Hanover*.

After his racing career was over, Bret became a successful sire: siring winners of $64,380,702.

When the champion horse died, Bret Hanover was originally buried at Castleton Farms, before his grave was relocated to Lexington Kentucky Horse Park. A statue was erected at Castleton Farms in honor of the champ, where it still stands today.

Adios Butler

Adios Butler (Adios—Debby Hanover) 1:54.3

$509,844

Adios Butler was the world's fastest harness horse (in his day) and was a native son of Roosevelt Raceway. He was coholder of the Roosevelt Raceway track record. He made his first and last start of his career over the famed Westbury oval.

Adios Butler's claim to fame was being the first horse ever to win the Little Brown Jug with a sub-two-minute mile.

Throughout his racing career, "The Butler" won the Messenger Stakes in stake and track record time. He was also the first pacer to win the Triple Crown of Harness Racing.

Adios Butler was voted "Horse of the Year" in 1960 and 1961. After his racing career was over, he retired to stud.

Adios Butler died at the age of twenty-seven.

Meadow Skipper

Meadow Skipper (Dale Frost—Countess Vivian)
1:55.2

$428,057

Anyone who knows anything about harness racing knows the name Meadow Skipper. "The Skipper" was a world champion or season champion every single year he raced. Meadow Skipper was not only a great racehorse, but one of the best sires in history.

He sired over 450 two-minute pacers, some who went on to be top-notch racehorses and sires, in their own right. These include Most Happy Fella, Albatross, and Ralph Hanover.

On The Road Again with Donny Sider

On the Road Again (Happy Motoring—Bye Bye Mollie) 1:51.4

$2,819,102

The story of the racehorse On the Road Again is every horse owner's dream. Gordon Rumpel, a retired automobile dealer from Calgary, Canada, purchased the horse as a yearling for $10,000.

By the time the horse retired, he earned $2.8 million for his owner.

Driven by Hall of Famer Buddy Gilmour, On the Road Again won the Federation Cup, the Cane Pace, the New Jersey Classic, the Levy Memorial, and the $1 million Meadowlands Pace.

He was Canada's Horse of the Year in 1984 and 1985, Three-Year-Old Pacing Colt in 1984, and Aged Pacing Colt in 1985.

After winning the race, the crowd would sing Willy Nelson's song "On the Road Again" during the victory celebration, while the horse proudly stood in the winners' circle.

On the Road Again retired with forty-four wins in sixty-one starts, racing over sixteen different racetracks. As a stallion, he was as successful as he was a racehorse.

He retired at Blue Chip Farms in New York. When he was retired from stud, he became very jealous of the other stallions for he wanted to remain the "king." The great horse died at the age of twenty-five.

Cardigan Bay

Cardigan Bay "The Television Star" (Tyrax—
Colwyn Bay)

$1,000,837

Cardigan Bay was foaled in New Zealand. During his outstanding racing career in Australia, Cardigan Bay rewrote record books. He was the first horse to win the Inter-Dominion Championship and the New Zealand Cup.

In 1962 and 1963, he won the prestigious Auckland Cup, and was inducted into the New Zealand Hall of Fame. "Cardy" (as he was nicknamed) was the first standardbred to win $1 million.

After getting worldwide recognition for his remarkable racing, he caught the attention of American driver/trainer Stanley Dancer.

Cardigan Bay won races in four countries—Canada, United States, New Zealand, and Australia.

At the ripe age of eight, Dancer leased the horse for $150,000 and brought him to America where he continued his amazing racing career. In 1966, Cardigan Bay won the Pace of the Century among many other stake races.

One time, Cardigan Bay appeared with his trainer, Stanley Dancer, on *The Ed Sullivan Show* as "The Million Dollar Horse."

In fact, Cardigan Bay was so famous that the country of New Zealand issued a postage stamp honoring this great pacer.

The champion horse raced until the age of twelve. Cardigan Bay lived out his retirement years in his native New Zealand.

6

The Founders Plate

The Founders Plate was an award of distinction. It was conceived to be a cherished prize in a tournament, designed to honor the man who was the founder of Roosevelt Raceway and the "Father of Modern Day Harness Racing," George Morton Levy. The award served as the ultimate competition for standardbred racehorses. To achieve the Founders Plate Award, along with the added $50,000 in prize money, a trotter or pacer had to win in successive years, the classic Roosevelt Raceway events for three- and four-year-olds.

A trotter had to win the Westbury Futurity at age two, the Dexter Cup at three, and the Realization Trot at four. A pacer had to do the same over three straight seasons, winning the Roosevelt Futurity at two, the Messenger at three, and the Realization Pace at four. The $50,000 added cash was shared among the owner, driver, trainer, and breeder. The owner would receive $35,000 plus the prestigious Founders Plate. The driver, trainer, and breeder/nominator each received $5,000 from Roosevelt Raceway. It took horses of exceptional ability to win the award named after a man of genuine greatness.

George Morton Levy founder of Roosevelt Raceway

7

Roosevelt Raceway: Dates to Remember

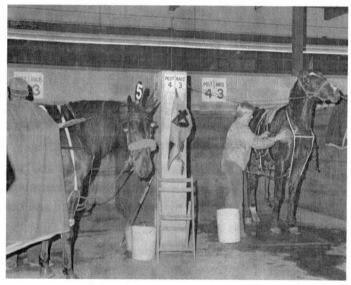

In the paddock

Loose Horse

The Forties

September 2, 1940: Roosevelt Raceway (Old Country Trotting Association) opens before 4,595 patrons who bet $40,742. A horse named Martha Lee wins first race with John (Red) Hanafin driving and pays $4.40.

October 5, 1940: 3,900 attend gateway night and bet $70,020—the best handle for the twenty-seven-night meet. The total gate for that meet was 75,749, and the total handle was $1,200,086.

May 28, 1941: The spring meet opens at Roosevelt, which had erected thirteen barns, a paddock, and a drivers' lounge.

June 6, 1941: The Daily Double is installed at Roosevelt Raceway.

July 2, 1941: A horse named Gilt Hanover, driven by Paul Vineyard, pays $239.60 to win. There were seventeen lucky winners. This would remain as the record win payoff.

September 13, 1941: The season closes with total attendance of 255,217; total wager $5,401,411

July 13, 1942: The Twilight Program starts at 5:30 p.m. Inaugurates 52 date wartime-restricted meeting. The meet draws 124,263. Total handle bet- $3,269,756.

July 29, 1943: Because of the war, racing was transferred to Empire City in Yonkers for the combined meetings of Roosevelt, Hamburg, and Saratoga Goshen.

May 29, 1944: Night racing returns to Roosevelt Raceway. It was a record opening handle of $220,035, bet by 7,084 patrons.

June 20, 1945: The one millionth fan, Carl Haracker, a contractor from Brooklyn, pays way into track.

June 8, 1946: The first $500,000 handle, as 14, 356 people bet $541,025.

July 3, 1946: The horse Doctor Spencer won one division of the inaugural American Trotting Championship. Summer Sun won the other respective division.

July 12, 1946: April Star wins the first National Pacing Derby.

Sept. 15, 1947: April Star wins the first Nassau Pace.

Aug. 14, 1948: The first million-dollar handle ($1,004,330).

August 14, 1949: Roosevelt Raceway celebrates ten years of being open.

The Fifties

July 20, 1951: Proximity, one of harness racing's all-time great mares, is retired in a track ceremony.

June 6, 1953: Hi-Lo's Forbes wins famed "Miracle Mile" in 1:58.3.

June 18, 1955: Adios Harry beats Adios Boy in 1:59.2 in a world-record race.

June 30, 1956: The first Messenger Stakes is won by Belle Acton with Billy Haughton driving.

Aug. 1, 1957: The $20,000,000 "Dream Track" opens.

August 16, 1957: The first $2,000,000 handle ($2,099,884).

Nov. 27, 1957: Triple-dead heat for win between Navy Song, Great Knight, and Flaxey Dream.

July 12, 1958: Driver Jimmy Cruise drives six straight winners for parimutuel track record.

August 1, 1959: International racing was introduced as French-bred Jamin wins the International Trot before 45,723 onlookers.

Aug. 28, 1959: Bye Bye Byrd sets world record for a mile pace on a half- mile strip in 1:57.4.

The Sixties

Aug. 20, 1960: The 1960 world record attendance of 54,861 see Holland's Hairos II take the second Roosevelt Raceway International.

June 30, 1961: Adios Butler equals world mile pace mark of 1:57.4.

July 15, 1961: 27,091 patrons see rain-soaked Su Mac Lad win the third International.

November 11, 1961: Adios Butler retires from racing winning the National Pacing Derby.

May 18, 1962: Messenger becomes the world's richest harness race ($169,430.93).

August 18, 1962: 53,279 people see Tie Silk win the fourth Roosevelt International.

September 28, 1962: Su Mac Lad sets 2:00 track mark for mile trot.

July 8, 1963: Roosevelt Raceway introduces the Twin Double to the Metropolitan area.

July 20, 1963: The fifth International goes to horse Su Mac Lad, before 40,153 onlookers.

October 14, 1963: Predawn fire destroys two barns and tragically kills twenty-seven racehorses.

December 7, 1963: Track record for a single night handle ($2,857,802).

April 15, 1964: Speedy Scot becomes the first Founders Plate winner.

August 22, 1964: Speedy Scot wins the sixth International before 46,614 spectators.

September 10, 1964: $172,726.80 Twin Double—a world mark for a $2 wager.

September 28, 1964: Roosevelt Raceway ends season with a record 3,229,243 patrons, who bet record $254,858,724. Average attendance per night (26,042) is a world mark.

May 13, 1965: Track introduces Westbury Tote's win and place exacta payoffs in running sequence of tote board.

June 17, 1965: Dartmouth wins Realization Trot and completes the second consecutive Founders Plate Sweep for Castleton Farm.

July 10, 1965: Pluvier III of Sweden scores upset victory in Roosevelt International before a crowd of 41,908. The winner pays $62.40.

November 19, 1965: Bret Hanover completes the Triple Crown for Pacers by taking $151,252 Messenger Stakes.

December 7, 1965: Su Mac Lad is retired in touching trackside ceremony.

May 24, 1966: New 366-foot Westbury Tote Electronic Board, flashing win, place, and show payoff possibilities, is unveiled.

May 28, 1966: Bret Hanover wins the Realization, becoming first pacer to sweep Founder's Plate.

July 9, 1966: Armbro Flight wins Roosevelt International Trot before 38,252 in breathtaking finish with France's Roqueine.

October 15, 1966: Levy and Johnson sell their controlling stock to the San Juan Racing Association. Levy stays on as chairman of the board.

October 29, 1966: Romeo Hanover completes the Triple Crown sweep by winning $169,885.24 Messenger Stakes, the richest harness race of all time.

May 16, 1967: Weil resigns as Roosevelt's president, stating the reason as "a disagreement over policy with other associates of the executive committee."

May 13, 1967: Romulus Hanover wins the $178,064 Messenger Stakes for Billy Haughton.

May 24, 1967: Roosevelt welcomes 50,000,000th patron.

July 5, 1967: George Morton Levy is inducted into the harness racing's Living Hall of Fame.

August 19, 1967: France's Roquepine captures the ninth Roosevelt International.

October 14, 1967: Flamboyant triumphs in the $183,463 Dexter Cup.

May 25, 1968: Cardigan Bay in dramatic 1:59.4 win as he nears the end of his grand career.

July 13, 1968: France's Roquepine registers the second successive Roosevelt International triumph.

October 26, 1968: Billy Haughton guides the horse Rum Customer to victory in the $189,018.15 Messenger's Stake (the world's richest harness race).

November 5, 1968: Over 8,500 in attendance as Nevele Pride victory.

December 14, 1968: Carmine Abbatiello clinches first Roosevelt driving title, edging Lucien Fontaine on the final night of the year.

October 1, 1969: Madison Square Garden buys out San Juan Racing Associations stock.

May 10, 1969: Bye Bye Sam is the upset Messenger winner as Stanley Dancer wins his first Messenger.

May 23, 1969: Herve Filion posts his first Roosevelt winner as Adios Waverly scores tremendous Realization Pace upset.

August 2, 1969: Nevele Pride sets world record for mile and a sixteenth in $88,670 Realization Trot with a time of 2:07.2.

August 9, 1969: Brothers Frank and Bill Popfinger become the first brothers to be in a dead-heat finish at Roosevelt.

August 23, 1969: The delayed Roosevelt International Trot goes to mare Une de Mai of France in a dramatic finish as Nevele Pride finishes second, before 39,052.

October 10, 1969: Lindy's Pride completes sweep of "Big Five" by taking the $173,455 Dexter Cup.

October 17, 1969: The total handle for the season reaches $283,846,318, a record.

The Seventies

January 3, 1970: The new du Pont Nordel rubberized surface makes its debut to critical acclaim at Roosevelt Raceway.

February 12, 1970: Del Insko becomes the fifth in harness racing history to score 2,500th victory.

February 28, 1970: The total handle for the night reaches $2,871,644—a record—as horse Good Chase registers 1:59.3 in mile race, an extraordinary accomplishment for this time of the year.

July 18, 1970: Fresh Yankee of Canada takes the Roosevelt International Trot, on her fourth try before 39,237.

October 23, 1970: John Chapman scores 2,500th lifetime victory.

November 7, 1970: Most Happy Fella completes sweep Triple Crown of Pacing by winning Messenger—the fifth Triple Crown sweep ever.

December 15, 1970: The first $3,000,000 total handle in Roosevelt history is reached by 24,600. The betting aggregates $3,118,346.

March 3, 1971: Roosevelt introduces the Big Triple Wager.

April 8, 1971: Off-track betting starts in New York with the first wager at Roosevelt.

May 22, 1971: Albatross wins the sixteenth Messenger Stakes in fast 2:00.2.

August 21, 1971: France's Une de Mai wins the International Trot again by barest of noses over Fresh Yankee of Canada. 34,247 were in attendance.

September 15, 1971: Preracing testing is first introduced in New York State at Roosevelt.

September 20, 1971: The Superfecta replaces the triple wager.

June 3, 1972: Albatross establishes the world record in Realization Pace and completes Founder's Plate sweep.

July 15, 1972: Speedy Crown defeats Fresh Yankee in International Trot, becoming the first US entrant since 1964 to annex global classic.

July 22, 1972: Speedy Crown turns back former International champions Une de Mai and Fresh Yankee (Canada) in unique $150,000 Challenge Match, and picks up largest purse check ever of $100,000.

October 31, 1972: Superfecta pays $32,874.80 for a Roosevelt record.

November 11, 1972: Silent Majority wins $154,733 Messengers Stake, making driver Billy Haughton the only four-time winner of the Three-Year-Old Pacing Classic.

November 22, 1972: Herve Filion breaks his own record when he records his 544th triumph of the season driving Eden All.

August 4, 1973: First afternoon racing program in Roosevelt's history attracts 13,612.

August 10, 1973: Sir Dalrae equals 1:57.4 track record in winning the $50,000 US Pacing Championship.

August 25, 1973: Delmonica Hanover, driven by John Chapman, beats country mate Spartan Hanover by a nose in the fifteenth International Trot.

December 20, 1973: Thirteen harness drivers arrested and indicted on allegedly fixing Superfectas.

December 26, 1973: The earliest opening in Roosevelt's history. The meet runs through March 2, 1974.

March 8, 1974: The famous Superfecta trial begins.

May 31, 1974: Otaro Hanover, driven by Herve Filion, establishes world record in $95,562 Realization Pace. Tar Heel stallion clocks 2:04.1 for mile and sixteenth standard after opening mile in 1:57.

July 10, 1974: France's Une de Mai, a two-time winner of the Roosevelt International Trot, officially retires at Roosevelt in a memorable and touching ceremony.

May 31, 1974: All drivers are found innocent of any wrongdoing in the Superfecta race fixing trial.

July 13, 1974: Delmonica Hanover wins the second straight Roosevelt International Trot for John Chapman, beating Canada's Keystone Gary by three-quarters of a length. The International purse was the largest in sports history—$200,000.

July 20, 1974: Italy's Dosson stuns Delmonica Hanover by winning the Challenge Match.

November 2, 1975: Armbro Omaha wins the $151,043 Messenger Stakes for Billy Haughton, nailing down three-year-old pacing championships. The 1:59.3 victory is Haughton's fifth Messenger win.

August 23, 1975: Savoir defeats Bellino II of France in second fastest Roosevelt International of all time with Del Insko driving.

October 11, 1975: Haughton wins his sixth Messenger Stakes with Brets Champ in the $154,222 event.

June 26, 1976: Tarport Hap shattered seventeen-year-old track pacing record with 1:57 win in the $50,000 US Pacing Championship.

July 10, 1976: France's Equileo captures the $200,000 Roosevelt International.

October 30, 1976: Billy Haughton does it again and wins his seventh Messenger Stakes with Windshield Wiper.

July 1, 1977: Keystone Pioneer establishes track trotting mark of 1:59.3.

July 16, 1977: Kash Minbar eclipses trotting standard win with a great performance of 1:58.3 in $50,000 American Trotting Championship.

July 19, 1977: George Morton Levy dies at his home after returning home from the night races. He was eighty-nine years old.

July 23, 1977: Delfo of Italy wins the $200,000 Roosevelt International Trot.

July 30, 1977: Kash Minbar wins the $50,000 mile and a half Challenge Cup in a world record of 3:01.3.

November 12, 1977: Governor Skipper matches stakes mark of 1:59.1 in the $159,155 Messenger Stakes.

August 12, 1978: A crowd of 30,277 witnessed US Cold Comfort tie the International mark of 2:31.3 for Peter Haughton, the youngest driver to ever win this race—at the age of twenty-three.

August 19, 1978: Governor Skipper sets track pacing mark of 1:56.3, with John Chapman driving for trainer Buck Norris.

October 28, 1978: Abercrombie wins the fastest Messenger of all time with 1:58.2 performance.

November 4, 1978: The first $200,000 George Morton Levy Memorial Pace goes to 24 to 1 long shot Sirota Anderson.

August 11, 1979: Peter Haughton wins his second successive Roosevelt International Trot with Doublemint, as defending champion is scratched after stall injury on the eve of the match.

August 18, 1979: France's Hillion Brillouard wins the Challenge Cup, overcoming an early break.

October 27, 1979: Hot Hitter wins the $180,225 Messenger Stakes for driver Henri Filion.

The Eighties

July 11, 1980: Niatross wins the Triple Crown by winning the $173,522 Messenger Stakes for Clint Galbraith.

August 16, 1980: Classical Way races from behind to win the $250,000 Roosevelt International Trot for John Simpson Jr.

August 23, 1980: Classical Way completes trots sweep in $100,000 Challenge Cup.

July 10, 1981: Sokys Atom wins the richest purse in Roosevelt history in the $512,800 Peter Haughton Memorial Pace.

July 12, 1981: Sunday night racing makes its debut at Roosevelt.

July 18, 1981: Melvins Strike with Joe Marsh Jr. driving equals track pacing record with a mile in 1:56.

July 25, 1981: France's Ideal Du Gazeau wins the $250,000 International over a fast closing Jorky.

July 31, 1981: Seahawk Hanover edges Eastern Skipper to win the $224,995 Messenger Stakes.

August 1, 1981: Ideal Du Gazeau and Jorky finish in a dead-heat for first in the $100,000 Challenge Trot Cup.

August 21, 1982: Mystic Park becomes the first three-year-old trotter ever to win the American Trotting Championship with Frank O'Mara driving.

August 28, 1982: Ideal Du Gazeau of France wins his second straight International Trot.

September 11, 1982: Big Band Sound and Billy Haughton equal the track record for two-year-old pacing colts with a time of 1:58.4.

October 16, 1982: Cam Fella wins the twenty-seventh edition of the Messenger Stakes for driver/trainer Pat Crowe.

November 4, 1982: Carmine Abbatiello wins his ninth Roosevelt driving title and sixth straight.

June 18, 1983: Ralph Hanover with Ron Waples driving wins the twenty-eighth edition of the Messenger Stakes.

July 8, 1983: Apache Circle wins the richest race ever in the history of Roosevelt, in the Peter Haughton Memorial with a purse of $559,800.

July 23, 1983: Ideal Du Gazeau becomes the first ever trotter to win three successive International Trots. The win also pushed Ideal's lifetime earnings over the $3 million mark, making him the richest standardbred of all time.

November 19, 1983: Cam Fella wins his twenty-fifth consecutive race, thus eclipsing Bret Hanover's record for consecutive wins in one season.

December 30, 1983: Rejean Daigneault edges Carmine Abbatiello 162–161 to win his first Roosevelt Driving Championship. His wife, Wendy , is the leading trainer.

April 27, 1984: Savvy Almahurst with Bill O'Donnell equals the track record of 1:56.4.

June 8, 1984: Speed Merchant with Tony Quartarolo driving win the $391,343 Dexter Cup.

July 16, 1984: The deal to sell the track is completed and the new owners, led by the investment firm of Evans and Hughes, purchase the track for $56 million.

August 25, 1984: France's Lutin D'Isigny wins the $250,000 Roosevelt International Trot, trotting the mile and a quarter event in a world record of 2:30.

September 29, 1984: Mickey McNichol guides Broadway Express to a track record for two-year-olds in the $611,800 Peter Haughton Memorial Pace, the richest race ever held at Roosevelt Raceway to date.

October 6, 1984: Troublemaker and Billy O'Donnell score a come from behind victory in the twenty-ninth edition of the $379,343 Messenger Stakes.

October 8, 1984: The largest payoff in New York racing history as Sweep Seven returns $199,618.

October 18, 1984: Mike Lachance becomes the first driver ever to record two hundred wins in one season at Roosevelt with his win by Able Tudor.

October 20, 1984: On the Road Again and Buddy Gilmour set a track record of 1:56 flat for three-year-old pacers.

March 17, 1985: Mike Lachance scores his 3,000th lifetime win with Delightful Pat.

March 26, 1985: Joe Marsh Jr. becomes the eighth driver in harness racing to record four thousand wins, as he wins with Durango.

June 22, 1985: Pershing Square and Billy O'Donnell win the Messenger Stakes. The gross purse was $485,560, making it the richest Messenger ever.

July 13, 1985: Buddy Gilmour drives On the Road Again to a track record of 1:55.2 in the George Morton Levy Memorial final.

July 20, 1985: Sandy Bowl and John Campbell wins the $100,000 American Trotting Championship.

July 27, 1985: Lutin D'Isigny wins his second straight International Trot, defeating Sandy Bowl of the United

States. It is the fifth straight win for the French, which gave them an 11–10 lead over the US overall.

July 31, 1985: Mike Lachance equals the Roosevelt Raceway dash record, winning six races in one program.

August 3, 1985: Lutin D'Isigny becomes the first trotter to sweep the Roosevelt International and Challenge Cup Trot in consecutive years.

November 30, 1985: On the Road Again makes his final start with a win in 2:00.3. He ends his career with forty-four wins in sixty-one starts and earnings of $2,819,108.

December 14, 1985: On the Road Again is retired in a trackside ceremony.

April 30, 1986: Dawn Patrol and Falcon Bret record the fastest dead heat in the history of Roosevelt in 1:58.1.

May 13, 1986: The first weekday doubleheader in Roosevelt's history.

June 4, 1986: "Pick 4" wagering debuts as an on-track bet.

August 9, 1986: Forrest Skipper and Lucien Fontaine win the US Pacing Championship, equaling the track record of 1:55.2.

August 16, 1986: Grades Singing and Herve Filion win the $100,000 American Trotting Championship. All eleven races go in 2:00 or faster—a track record.

August 23, 1986: Norway's Habib wins the International Trot.

October 4, 1986: Amity Chef wins the $333,762 Messenger Stakes for John Campbell, upsetting Barberry Spur's bid for a Triple Crown.

October 26, 1986: Mike Lachance drives Blaze Blaze to victory, his 638th win of the year—a new all-time record, besting Herve Filion's standard. Lachance scored 359 winners at Roosevelt in 1986—a track record.

August 22, 1987: Callit of Sweden wins the $200,000 International Trot, which will be the last International raced at Roosevelt Raceway.

October 24, 1987: Roosevelt Raceway starts cutting its cost by limiting the hours on the training track, and limiting the hours of the barn area to 6:30 a.m. to 5:00 p.m.

June 15, 1988: Majestic Andrew wins the last race to ever be conducted at Roosevelt Raceway with driver Rejean Daigneault driving.

July 15, 1988: It is announced that Roosevelt Raceway is closed for good.

July 29, 1988: Horsemen offer to purchase Roosevelt Raceway, but the offer is rejected.

September 10, 1988: George Steinbrenner offers to purchase Roosevelt Raceway for $51 million. Again, the offer is rejected.

2000: The Roosevelt Raceway grandstand is torn down.

8

Statistics and Track Records

Roosevelt Raceway
Year-By-Year Attendance Totals

Year	Race Days	Total	Average Night	Highest Night	Date
1940	27	75175	2784	4687	09/02/40
1941	58	255217	4400	8351	05/30/41
1942	52	124263	2390	4241	08/15/42
1943		At Empire			
1945	94	847504	9016	12118	09/08/45
1946	122	1173961	9623	25563	07/03/46
1947	118	1470552	12462	26986	08/22/47
1948	136	1983764	14587	28219	07/24/48
1949	147	2281534	15521	30535	05/21/49
1950	105	1563857	14894	25173	06/07/50
1951	106	1762521	16628	29324	08/11/51

1952	108	1746217	16169	29026	05/30/52
1953	107	2017939	18859	35048	08/15/53
1954	106	1945055	18349	30418	07/17/54
1955	115	2131650	18536	31603	04/30/55
1956	104	1962963	18874	31247	07/07/56
1957	105	2400774	22864	50337	08/17/57
1958	105	2569312	24470	39480	05/30/58
1959	104	2293203	22050	45723	08/01/59
1960	104	2490043	23943	50861	08/20/60
1961	115	2555867	22225	40223	06/03/61
1962	105	2477057	23591	53279	08/18/62
1963	123	2825104	22968	40153	07/20/63
1964	124	3229243	26042	46614	08/22/64
1965	133	2983046	22429	41908	07/10/65
1966	154	3088824	20057	38527	07/09/66
1967	144	3023299	20995	41671	08/12/67
1968	150	2865617	19104	38480	07/13/68
1969	143	2992485	20926	39669	08/02/69
1970	155	3077890	19857	39237	07/18/70
1971	142	3013209	21220	39247	08/21/71
1972	154	2625336	17048	34645	07/15/72
1973	148	2555903	17270	33325	08/25/73
1974	164	2600996	15859	37407	08/23/74
1975	137	2284636	16676	33297	08/23/75
1976	169	2252672	13329	33929	07/10/76
1977	156	1794536	11503	26795	07/23/77
1978	147	1706348	11608	30277	08/12/78
1979	154	1627394	10567	23330	08/11/79
1980	156	1504288	9643	24931	08/16/80
1981	146	1290127	8836	20337	07/25/81

1982	156	1361771	8729	20713	08/28/82
1983	159	1247787	7848	19305	07/23/83
1984	157	1087036	6923	17161	08/25/84
1985	174	969079	5569	13613	07/27/85
1986	183	835474	4565	12499	08/23/86
1987	No data				
1988	No data				
Total	5844	89377776	15294	54861	08/20/60

Roosevelt Raceway
Track Records By-Age-And-Sex

PACERS

Age	Horse	Driver	Time	Date
2 yr. Colt	Broadway Express	M. McNichol	1.58	09/29/84
2 yr. Filly	Valentina	W. Haughton	1.59	07/03/85
2 yr. Gelding	Prince Papide N	J. Joanisse	1.59.2	11/02/78
3 yr. Colt	Pershing Square	W. O'Donnell	1.55.2*	06/22/85
3 yr. Filly	Naughty But Nice	T.Haughton	1.56.4	08/17/84
3 yr. Gelding	Mr. Escort	R.Remmen	1.56.4	10/27/84
3 yr. Gelding	Long Tall	J. Patterson, Jr.	1.56.4	09/20/86
3 yr. Gelding	Pacific Dream	J. Marsh, Jr.	1.56.4	10/18/86
4 yr. Horse	On The Road Again	W. Gilmour	1.55.2*	07/13/85
4 yr. Horse	Falcon Seelster	T. Harmer	1.55.2*	06/13/86
4 yr. Horse	Forrest Skipper	L. Fontaine	1.55.2*	08/09/86
4 yr. Mare	Tarport Hap	J. Chapman	1.57	06/26/76
4 yr. Gelding	Division Street	J. Patterson, Jr.	1.56.4	05/12/84
Aged Horse	Mr. Dalrae	D. Magee	1.56.2	08/11/84
Aged Horse	Flying Rich	C. Abbatiello	1.56.2	09/27/86

Aged Mare	Samshu Bluegrass	M. Lachance	1.57.2	05/20/86
Aged Gelding	Docs Fella	M. Lachance	1.56.2	10/20/84

At Distances Other Than One Mile

Distance	Horse	Driver	Time	Date
½	Miss Emmadale	P. Vineyard	1.00.2	06/03/44
9/16th	Little To Ri	J.Campbell	1.04**	09/16/80
¾	Luther Hanover	J. Jordan	1.31.1/2	06/01/41
	Stoneridge Direct	M. Dennison	1.31.1/2	06/09/41
13/16	Adios Boy	H. Camden	1.36**	08/06/54
1-1/16th	Otaro Hanover	Her. Filion	2.04.2**	05/31/74
1-1/8th	Tru Single G	S. Werner	2.24.1/4	09/11/45
1-1/4th	Irvin Paul	C. King	2.29.3	09/01/62
1 and ½	Tarquinius	G. Sholty	3.03	09/12/64
2 miles	Scottish Pence	W. Smart	4.131/2	08/02/51

* Track Pacing Record
** World Record

TROTTERS

Age	Horse	Driver	Time	Date
2 yr. Colt	Workaholic	J Johnson	Time 2.02.4	09/19/84
2 yr. Filly	Armbro Devona	J. Marsh, Jr.	Time 2.02.3	09/11/84
2 yr. Gelding	Prince Jamie	F. Spencer	Time 2.06.1	09/29/59
3 yr. Colt	Joie De Vie	W. Gilmour	1.59.2	06/24/83
3 yr. Colt	Speed Merchant	A. Quartarolo	1.59.2	06/08/84
3 yr. Filly	Meadowmiss Hanover	B. Steall	1.59.3	09/04/86
3 yr. Gelding	Eric G.	L. Fontaine	Time 2.02.3	08/16/79
4 yr. Horse	Sandy Bowl	J. Campbell	1.58.4	07/20/85
4 yr. Mare	Grades Singing	Her. Filion	1.58.2*	08/16/86
4 yr. Gelding	Benny T.	M. Lachance	2.00.4	09/26/86
Aged Horse	Kash Minbar	E. Cruise	1.58.3	07/16/77
Aged Horse	Keystone Pioneer	W. Haughton	1.59.3	07/01/77
Aged Gelding	Statelys Pride	W. Gilmour	1.59	07/30/83

At Distances Other Than One Mile

Distance	Horse	Driver	Time	Date
½ a mile	Tact	C. Hodgins	Time 1.03.2	05/31/44
9/16th of a mile	Robert Hanover	C. Dill	1.09	09/06/40
	Harry Dewey	C. Fleming	1.09	09/10/40

	Prince Martinique	C. Mabrey	1.09	08/19/42
	Happy	C. Mason	1.09	08/22/42
¾ of a mile	Milestone	W. Smart	1.32**	06/30/41
1 mile & 3/16th	Katie Key	C. Hodgins	1.37.1	07/30/54
1 mile & 1/16th	Nevele Pride	S. Dancer	2.07.2**	08/02/69
1 mile & 1/8th	Count Up	N. Philips	2.26	09/26/45
1 mile & 1/4th	Lutin D'Isigny	J. P. Andre	2.30**	08/25/84
1 and ½	Kash Minbar	E. Cruise	3.01.3**	07/30/77
2 miles	Pronto Don	B. Schue	Time 4.10.4	09/13/51

* Track Trotting Record
** World Record

Roosevelt Raceway
Year-By-Year Handle Totals

Year	Race Days	Total	Average	Highest Night	Date	Per Capita	State Revenue
1940	27	$1,200,866.00	$44,448.00	$69,018.00	09/28/40	$15.96	$64,818.67
1941	58	$5,401,411.00	$93,128.00	$153,432.00	09/13/41	$23.98	$292,725.67
1942	52	$3,269,756.00	$62,880.00	$133,172.00	08/15/42	$26.31	$176,262.49
1943	At Empire						
1944	73	$15,078,831.00	$206,559.00	$314,938.00	09/02/44	$37.02	$819,994.63
1945	94	$28,419,887.00	$303,105.00	$454,675.00	08/10/45	$33.62	$1,543,934.47
1946	122	$53,839,659.00	$441,309.00	$810,708.00	07/03/46	$45.86	$2,896,005.44
1947	118	$62,940,379.00	$553,393.00	$964,709.00	08/22/47	$42.80	$3,376,598.01
1948	136	$88,491,899.00	$650,676.00	$1,067,389.00	09/11/48	$44.61	$4,314,139.23
1949	147	$95,283,088.00	$648,184.00	$1,076,601.00	08/05/49	$41.76	$4,618,919.47
1950	105	$68,879,748.00	$655,998.00	$983,104.00	08/12/50	$44.05	$4,299,802.79
1951	106	$83,469,742.00	$787,450.00	$1,124,926.00	08/11/51	$47.36	$5,341,429.78
1952	108	$95,338,401.00	$882,763.00	$1,251,642.00	09/11/52	$54.60	$6,464,905.02
1953	107	$117,783,400.00	$1,100,779.00	$1,713,309.00	08/15/53	$58.37	$8,134,781.46
1954	106	$109,156,431.00	$1,029,778.00	$1,432,404.00	08/14/54	$56.11	$10,380,268.00
1955	115	$126,465,478.00	$1,099,700.00	$1,592,144.00	05/14/55	$59.33	$12,203,687.29
1956	104	$122,338,108.00	$1,176,328.00	$1,661,107.00	05/19/56	$62.32	$11,940,984.41
1957	105	$166,252,334.00	$1,583,355.00	$2,388,674.00	08/17/57	$69.25	$14,151,455.56
1958	105	$184,260,373.00	$1,754,861.00	$2,502,196.00	05/28/58	$71.72	$15,224,434.04
1959	104	$165,110,362.00	$1,587,600.00	$2,692,585.00	11/30/59	$72.00	$14,060,785.99
1960	104	$183,282,257.00	$1,762,332.00	$2,730,113.00	08/20/60	$73.61	$14,654,737.00
1961	115	$193,475,614.00	$1,682,397.00	$2,706,275.00	11/30/61	$75.69	$15,699,979.48
1962	105	$189,713,964.00	$1,806,800.00	$2,793,596.00	08/18/62	$76.59	$17,524,327.89
1963	123	$214,942,753.00	$1,747,502.00	$2,857,802.00	08/18/63	$76.08	$21,725,659.72
1964	124	$254,858,724.00	$2,055,312.00	$2,722,610.00	12/07/64	$78.92	$26,143,791.77
1965	133	$244,373,336.00	$1,837,393.00	$2,743,772.00	12/15/65	$81.92	$24,866,635.76
1966	154	$268,296,838.00	$1,742,187.00	$2,764,072.00	12/15/66	$86.86	$27,778,612.80
1967	144	$270,758,022.00	$1,880,264.00	$2,734,702.00	08/12/67	$89.56	$28,083,010.53
1968	150	$267,832,084.00	$1,785,547.00	$2,683,020.00	03/03/68	$93.46	$28,445,039.71
1969	143	$283,846,318.00	$1,984,939.00	$2,817,870.00	04/26/69	$94.73	$30,928,080.55

1970	155	$310,923,401.00	$2,005,957.00	$3,118,346.00	12/15/70	$101.02	$34,572,819.00
1971	142	$297,815,752.00	$2,097,294.00	$2,846,734.00	08/21/71	$98.84	$34,093,993.39
1972	154	$289,201,102.00	$1,877,929.00	$2,752,686.00	02/12/72	$110.16	$32,558,632.63
1973	148	$280,889,037.00	$1,897,899.00	$2,747,727.00	04/07/73	$109.52	$31,284,979.10
1974	164	$314,250,315.00	$1,916,160.00	$3,077,946.00	07/13/74	$120.82	$34,627,327.00
1975	137	$272,432,122.00	$1,988,556.00	$2,866,747.00	05/17/75	$119.25	$30,217,082.42
1976	169	$289,007,899.00	$1,710,106.00	$2,951,254.00	07/10/76	$128.29	$31,257,012.51
1977	156	$234,793,289.00	$1,505,085.00	$2,396,698.00	08/13/77	$130.34	$19,829,303.00
1978	147	$239,812,469.00	$1,631,377.00	$2,945,120.00	08/12/78	$140.54	$20,169,788.00
1979	154	$253,373,413.00	$1,645,282.00	$2,686,537.00	08/11/79	$155.50	$21,573,433.90
1980	156	$243,860,959.00	$1,573,297.00	$2,669,887.00	08/16/80	$162.11	$20,856,390.79
1981	146	$212,269,291.00	$1,453,899.00	$2,325,416.00	07/25/81	$164.53	$15,749,041.64
1982	156	$233,179,426.00	$1,494,740.00	$2,483,378.00	08/28/82	$171.24	$15,146,970.54
1983	159	$210,491,394.00	$1,323,845.00	$2,050,740.00	07/23/83	$168.69	$13,533,107.30
1984	157	$191,572,153.00	$1,220,204.00	$2,040,726.00	08/25/84	$176.23	$12,110,440.97
1985	174	$186,197,490.00	$1,070,100.00	$1,852,080.00	08/03/85	$192.15	$7,644,261.98
1986	183	$174,836,797.00	$955,392.00	$1,765,085.00	08/23/86	$209.27	$4,601,996.00
1987 No data							
1988 No data							
Total	5844	$7,743,207,612.00	$1,324,987.00	$3,118,346.00	12/15/70	$86.63	$700,259,211.45

9

Freddie's Trivia

Playing "Freddie's Trivia" is a fun way of finding out how much you know about Roosevelt Raceway, the drivers, and the horses during "the golden years."

1. Which Roosevelt driver won the dash four times and the percentage title two times?
2. Who was the first Roosevelt Raceway driver to win six races on one card?
3. What year did Roosevelt Raceway have its very first "million-dollar handle?"
4. In driver/trainer Frank Popfinger's own words, how many starts did he say it took for him to win his first race at Roosevelt Raceway?
5. How many tries did it take Buddy Gilmour to establish himself at Roosevelt Raceway?
6. Who offered Del Insko a job as a trainer when he was starting out in the business?
7. What was the name of the favorite restaurant to most drivers and trainers at Roosevelt Raceway?
8. What year did Del Insko win his 2,500th win?
9. What year did the fifty-millionth patron go to Roosevelt?
10. Name the three trainers who lost their race horses in the 1963 fire.
11. Roosevelt Raceway advertised itself as what two words: _____ _____ of harness racing?
12. Name the two brothers registered as the first Roosevelt Raceway brothers' dead heat.
13. How many triple dead heats have there been at Roosevelt Raceway?
14. Name the horse that holds the record for the fastest Roosevelt Racing trotting mile.

15. Which horse holds the record for the most starts in the International Trot?
16. What country holds the record for the most wins in the International Trot with different horses?
17. What year was the first two-minute-mile recorded at Roosevelt Raceway?
18. At Roosevelt Raceway, name the pacer who has recorded the most 2:00 or faster miles. How many?
19. At Roosevelt Raceway, which trotter has recorded the most 2:00 or better miles and how many?
20. What driver has the most two-minute or faster miles?
21. How many times have the races in a single card gone 2:00 or better at Roosevelt Raceway?
22. What trotter was the first to record a 2:00 mile at Roosevelt Raceway, and what year was it?
23. What driver holds the most wins at Roosevelt Raceway?
24. What driver had the most Roosevelt Raceway wins in one year?
25. Four drivers have won six races on one card at Roosevelt Raceway. Who are they?
26. What was the price of the highest horse ever claimed at Roosevelt Raceway?
27. What was the highest purse ever offered at Roosevelt?
28. Roosevelt Raceway had three tracks: the main track, the training track, and a jogging track. What did everyone call the jogging track?
29. The record for the most money wagered on a single horse in one race at Roosevelt Raceway is $176,916. Who was that horse?
30. What is the time of the fastest Roosevelt Raceway dead heat?

31. What driver has won the most annual Roosevelt Raceway driving titles?
32. What is the record for attendance at Roosevelt Raceway?
33. How many times did Roosevelt Raceway have fifty thousand or more people in attendance.?
34. How many times did the Roosevelt Raceway handle go over $3 million?
35. Who won the first Roosevelt Raceway International Trot in 1959?
36. Name the three drivers who have won the Roosevelt Raceway International on three different horses?
37. How many times has the USA won the Roosevelt International?
38. What country has won the most Roosevelt Raceway International?
39. What driver has won the most Roosevelt Raceway International?
40. How many horses from the USA in the same year have won the American Trotting Championship, the International, and the Challenge Cup?
41. What year did OTB (off-track betting) start?
42. Who were the two founders of Roosevelt Raceway?
43. In the famous superfecta trial, a witness mistakenly identified what sports writer as cashing superfecta tickets?
44. What was the name of the first horse to win a race at Roosevelt Raceway?
45. What number one television show taped an episode at Roosevelt?

Trivia Answers

1. William Haughton was the leading percentage driver in the years 1957 and 1965, and was the leading dash winning driver in 1956, 1957, 1958, and 1962.
2. Jimmy Cruise, July 12, 1958.
3. August 14, 1948 ($1,004,330).
4. At the Roosevelt Raceway Reunion in 2009, Frank Popfinger said that it took forty starts before he won his first race.
5. Buddy Gilmour said he tried four times to establish himself at Roosevelt.
6. Joe O'Brien.
7. The Gam Wah.
8. February 12, 1970.
9. May 24, 1967.
10. William Hudson, Anthony Abbatiello, and Howard Beissinger.
11. World Capital
12. Frank and Billy Popfinger.
13. Three, one each for win, place, and show.
14. Grades Singing, 1:58.2. August 16, 1982, Herve Fillion driving.
15. Fresh Yankee (six) 1967–1972.
16. USA (eight)
   - 1961 and 1963, Su Mac Lad
   - Speedy Scot
   - Speedy Crown
   - 1973 and 1974 Delmonica Hanover
   - Savoir
   - Cold Comfort

- Doublemint
- Classical Way
17. June 6, 1953, Hi Los Forbes (2:00), H. Clukey driving.
18. Doc's Fella (fifteen),
19. Grades Singing (four).
20. Mike Lachance (196).
21. Two times. June 29, 1985 (ten races) and August 16, 1986 (eleven races).
22. Su Mac Lad (2:00), September 28, 1962. Stanley Dancer driving.
23. Carmine "The Red Man" Abbatiello (2,575).
24. Mike Lachance (359), 1986.
25. Jimmy Cruise, Buddy Gilmour, and Mike Lachance.
26. Watchit Skipper ($125,000), November 29,1984.
27. $611,800 for the Peter Haughton Memorial, September 29, 1984.
28. The jogging track was referred to as "The Hole."
29. Bret Hanover in the 1965 Messenger.
30. 1:58.1 with Dawn Patrol (Sonny Patterson) and Falcon Bret (Mike Lachance) on April 30, 1986.
31. Carmine Abbatiello (nine) 1968 to 1970 and 1977 to 1982.
32. 54,861 on August 20, 1960.
33. Three times on August 17, 1957, August 20, 1960, and August 18, 1962.
34. Twice, December 15, 1970, and July 13, 1974.
35. Jamin of France.
36. Peter Haughton (Cold Comfort in 1978, and Doublemint in 1979), Jean Rene Gougeon (Roquepine in 1968 and Une De Mai in 1969 and 1971), and Joe O'Brien (Armbro Flight in 1966 and Fresh Yankee in 1970).

37. The USA has won ten times.
38. France with eleven.
39. Three each, Jean Rene Gougeon of France and Eugene Lefevre of France.
40. Three: Speedy Crown—1972; Savoir—1975; Classical Way—1980.
41. April 8, 1971.
42. George Morton Levy and Robert Johnson.
43. Tony Sisti of *Newsday*.
44. Martha Lee on September 2, 1940.
45. The *I Love Lucy* show in 1957.

Testimonials and Tributes

Below are testimonials and tributes that were given to us from special people. Several of them at one time had a very important part in the operating or racing at Roosevelt Raceway. Others experienced special, personal times at Roosevelt which left a huge impact in their life and will always remain in their hearts.

> Having spent so much of my younger life 'under the lights and under the stars' at Roosevelt Raceway, where it all began, I can barely wait to read the definitive book on the great racetrack by the acknowledged and acclaimed author, Victoria Howard, and her co-authors Billy Haughton and Freddie Hudson.
>
> I know how much research has gone into this project and I have every confidence it will indeed be the definitive story of where nighttime harness racing truly began.
>
> —Bob Marks (Horse breeder, writer, public relations at Roosevelt Raceway)

Where it all began—Where it is today—The World Capital of Harness Racing." That was the opening line every night from the announcer's booth at Roosevelt Raceway.

I inherited that line from Jack E. Lee, who I succeeded in 1985 and continued until the end came in 1988. Roosevelt gave me great some of the greatest memories I have from the sport we all love: Harness Racing.

So many memories! I watched Colonial upset Albatross. I watched the likes of Tropic Song, Meadow Paige, Bossman Lobell, Chris Time, Lavender Laddie, Pammy Lobell, Commander Dell, Chief Crazy Legs...I could go on forever.

In my announcing years I became friends with many of the greats of the day. I got to rub elbows with the greats and scratch the heads of the horses I loved. I believe this was the golden era of Harness Racing, and I am very glad to be able to say that I was a small part of it.

—Jerry Glantz (Track announcer and owner/breeder)

It was a fantastic feeling racing there. When I first came to Roosevelt Raceway it was intimidating. After being there, you felt like you were part of history. It was a fantastic place: the lights and the noise of the crowd.

Everyone in New York knew me. I would walk down the street and person after person would stop and ask me for my autograph.It was just a great experience—the greatest ever!

Everyone in harness racing wanted to race there. It was the Major League of Harness Racing.

—Lucien Fontaine (World-class harness driver/owner)

I first came aware of Roosevelt Raceway while I was living and working in Xenia, Ohio with fellow Xenian Stephen Phillips, who invented the mobile starting gate in 1946.

In the years to follow I would read and hear the stories of JAMIN winning the first International Trot; the early years of racing greats Stanley Dancer and Billy Haughton; of Stan Bergstein and Spencer Ross; and their weekly "Racing from Roosevelt" show—just to name a few of the many harness racing stars from Roosevelt Raceway.

Those wonderful memories have always been etched in my mind. The impact of world class racing at Roosevelt was such an influence to the sport of harness racing that can never be duplicated. This book has been long anticipated by myself and many others who never had the opportunity to attend the races at Roosevelt.

—Roger Huston (Racetrack announcer,
Hall of Fame Sportswriter)

It was back on September 2, 1940, that the Old Country Trotting Association held the very first pari-mutuel event at Roosevelt Raceway.

A 6 to 5 favorite won that first race held on their half-mile oval paving way for Roosevelt Raceway, itself, to become the favorite venue for, literally, millions of racing fans for almost a half century.

From the now long forgotten Martha Lee, who won the first race for driver John Hanafin, to the May 24, 1946 introduction of the Phillips mobile starting gate to the greatest of horses and horsemen (women, too), Roosevelt Raceway attracted them all…and rightfully so.

From the American Trotting Association events to the famed Roosevelt International to the National Pacing Derby to the Messenger...from Doctor Spencer to Bye Bye Byrd to Bret Hanover and Cardigan Bay on the pace...to Proximity, Su Mac Lad, Speedy Crown and the artichoke eating Jamin on the trot...and, of course, Stanley, Billy, Herve, the "Red Man" and toothpick Del, this incredible book covers all of it...and more.

Roosevelt Raceway, itself, may be gone, but this grand book will keep the memories alive and vivid for all of us who are enamored with our great sport and its legends.

—John Berry (Communicators Hall of Fame journalist)

Most cherished childhood memories revolve around parks, playgrounds, seashores or a myriad of other family oriented locations, but many of my childhood revolved around a magical and exciting place...a racetrack, Roosevelt Raceway.

Everything about the raceway was fascinating to me—the grandstand, the stable area, the Cloud Casino, the maintenance building (from where we watched the races when we were too young to go to the Club House) and the treat of all treats, the paddock area! Memories of my childhood spent at the raceway will forever hold a very special place in my heart.

The raceway was significantly important to many people for many reasons, but none more so than my father.

The triumph and success of Roosevelt was especially dear to him since building and establishing the track was not without many struggles in the early days. Through it all he maintained a vision of something extraordinary. This vision did indeed become a reality and Roosevelt Raceway emerged as the extraordinary place we all remember and love.

The love and pride my father felt for Roosevelt Raceway and all the people and horses who made it great was enormous. I am grateful beyond words to all the men and women who continue to honor and remember Roosevelt Raceway because by doing so you allow my father's dream to live on.

—CeCe Levy (Daughter of Roosevelt Raceway founder George Morton Levy)

It was 1951. I was newly married. It was a glorious time. Bill's stable was just inside the stable gate. It's funny because I can still remember the name of every horse in our stable and exactly which stall they called home.

After training in the morning everything was raked up and put away. The harness and equipment were cleaned and hanging in their bags; the trunks were wiped down and shining. All the grooms were proud to be in the W.R. Haughton Stable, and it showed.

In the evening when I went to the races the drivers and owners' wives dressed up like we were going out to a fancy restaurant. We wore dresses, high heels and sometimes hats. (No jeans, sneakers, or t-shirts in that era.) It was elegant and sophisticated.

I can remember that many nights the entrance gates were closed because there was such a big crowd. There was no room for any more cars—even though the parking lot was huge. I really miss the atmosphere, class, excitement and beauty of it all.

They had wonderful fans—many had become friends for life. Bill was highly respected as a driver by the fans and was very popular. All the employees of Roosevelt Raceway were very professional, friendly and polite. They made everyone that went there feel welcomed.

The drivers and their families were all good friends, and they socialized regularly; but once they were on the racetrack and the starting gate pulled away, it was every man for himself. The only goal was to win!

I am so happy to have been a part of the wonderful era of Roosevelt Raceway from 1951- 1986 for me.

Thank you Victoria, Billy and Freddie for sharing the history of how this track was started and the great people, horses and stories that were enjoyed by so many.

—Dorothy B. Haughton (owner/trainer/breeder/ driver and wife of Billy Haughton)

I spent most of my weekend and summer days at the track. I graduated from high school in 1988—the same month they announced Roosevelt Raceway was closing. I found out they closed when we pulled up to the barn area and I saw John Slattery from the news outside the track kitchen. There were other news crews there but I only recognized him.

A couple of weeks before the Roosevelt International Trot—(the banner advertising the race) that stretched across Merrick Ave, from 'the hole' training track to Eisenhower Park.

My grandfather (Mike Sr.) was in barn LL—when the International horses came in, they were in the last barn on the left side (when heading to the training track). A temporary fence was put up and they had 24 hr. security. I would go up to the fence and watch the horses—and I especially sought out IDEAL DU GAZEAU every year.

Lou Meitteinis' father (or was it uncle?) had the barber shop in the building at the middle of the barn area. I would go there for a bottle of Coke and play video games (Space Invaders and Asteroids).

All the old timers would be playing cards and smoking cigars. The wall next to the pay phone had all the important phone numbers written on it: shippers, Roosevelt Raceway extensions, farms, drivers, and trainers.

I made a few trips to Vinny Aurigemma's barn to visit DOC'S FELLA after everyone had left for the day—he was my favorite pacer.

BOBBO was my favorite trotter. I loved Jack Lee call him "BOOOOOObbo" during the race.

Jack was the greatest race announcer ever. He always gave the local sports scores during the races. I always wanted to know the scores of the playoff games when the Islanders were winning their fourth straight Stanley Cup.

Bobby Vitrano was listed to drive KASH PERSUASION in 1978 and he didn't show up, so the judges had to name a driver from the race before—-when me and my grandfather heard Jack Lee announce "In the second race KASH PERSUASION will be driven by Billy Haughton, we were so excited! We looked at each other in amazement. He had never driven one of our horses before. He finished 2nd and after he got the horse, he told my grandfather if he knew what he had under him, he would've won!

My favorite races to see were the International Trot and the Messenger Stakes.

1980 Messenger Stakes—the great Niatross. This was HUGE for me. I couldn't wait to see him in person. I remember the display that was built that lit up when he won. The front display said "Niatross" and I believe the one in the back said "Triple Crown Championship," or something very close to that.

My favorite race was always the International. My first one was 1978 (7 years old) and COLD COMFORT won. WE sat in the owners section (blue seats) and my grandfather was yelling "come on Peter" (Peter Haughton) through the stretch. Then he pointed out that he fell out of the seat after the finish. Everyone was laughing.

'CAM FELLA' and 'ON THE ROAD AGAIN' were two of my favorites to watch. They always brought in a big crowd and had so many fans. I still have my "CAM FELLA—THE PACING MACHINE" button that was given out at Roosevelt Raceway.

Dennis had some really HOT girls working for him. They were about 20 years old, I was 17—I spent many days staring across at those girls!

—Mike Lizzi (Track photographer at Yonkers Raceway, standardbred racing advocate)

About the Authors

Victoria M. Howard

Victoria is a ten times published author. She has written books on relationships, self-help, and has recently written a trilogy for children called *The Adventures of Max*.

In Book One, Max the Bolognese dog befriends a Standardbred race horse named Molly. Through the teaching of these animals, children learn the correct values and morals needed in life.

Victoria has won several beauty pageants and once represented her state in "The Mrs. USA Pageant."

In 2012, she was awarded "VIP Woman of the Year" by Who's Who Worldwide.

Today Victoria hosts her own radio talk show and pens a column in a local paper called "Dear Victoria."

She has owned, trained and bred racehorses for forty years and once co-owned EFISHNC who was "The Two-Year-Old Filly Pacer of the Year."

Throughout the years she has been the proud "mama" to over one hundred Standardbred racehorses, which is her passion and true love.

Billy Haughton

Billy Haughton is the eldest son of William R. Haughton, arguably the greatest trainer/driver in the history of the sport of Harness Racing.

Billy has immersed in the business of harness racing throughout his life—from grooming and training—to stable administration, and then ownership of a horseman's insurance agency.

He has been insuring horsemen and horsewomen, horses and farms, etc. for the past thirty-seven years, and looks to support and promote the sport in any way possible.

He states: "The writing of this book will bring to life and share the heartbeat, drama and excitement shared by many. It combines the history of Roosevelt's beginning with the stories of those great days spent in the rapidly developing area surrounding, and including "The Dream Track" Roosevelt Raceway.

Several more volumes would be needed to detail those days and recognize all that were there, and to share their stories and fond memories. This is a start, and I hope you enjoy it to the finish.

Freddie Hudson

Fred is a third-generation trainer/driver who considers his teachers and mentors his dad (Billy Hudson), Clint Hodgins, Jimmy Jordan, Joe O'Brien, George Phalen, Billy and Alan Myer, and he was the protégé of Del Insko.

Fred is best remembered as the head trainer of the Del Insko Stable and has trained or helped develop such horses as Noble Jade, Fresh Yankee, Atashy, Romeo Allegro, Stylish Major, Steady Success, Mariposa, Blu Fireball, Weikers Hope, Alba Counsel, and many more.

Outside of harness racing, Fred has held positions in marketing, with several companies with titles ranging from director to CEO.

He was the Director of International Sales for W. Quinn and Associates who developed and produced the world's number one software storage application. He was also the VP of Sales and Marketing for LGA, and was the CEO of Techniksoft.

Currently Fred is an advisor to several owners and trainers and is using his marketing skills to help promote and save the harness racing industry. He is a member of USHWA and was also the co-host of the radio show North America Harness Updates.

He has also organized and hosted several harness racing events, including the Roosevelt Raceway Reunions.

Acknowledgments

While writing this book, there were many generous people who provided important information, stories, and facts which were used in this book. Below is a list of people we would like to thank for their time and help:

Roger Huston
Robert Goldstein
Dorothy Haughton
Bob Marks
Lucien Fontaine
Jerry Glantz
Mike Lizzi
Barry Lefkowitz
Mick Bazsuly
Bobby Vitrano
Carmine Abbatielo
Bobby Hiel
Dean Hoffman
Bill Heller
Steve Wolf
Alan Prince
Ted Black
Ellen Harvey
Hollywood "Bob" Heyden
John Berry
Mike Santa Maria
Maxine Pullman
Eric Abbatiello
Peter Cashman
Bobby Rahner
Janet Terhune

Joe Faraldo
John Miritello
Frank Galante
Ester Balanzano
Jeffrey Bergelt
Jim Champion
Tom Faulhaber
Frank Tagariello
Chris Tully
Dan Myer
Sherri (Twiggy) Lane
Beverly Anne Newkirk
Gino Martucci
Del Insko
Ken McNutt
Judy Bokman
John Manzi
Heather Moffett
Wendy Paton
Rebecca Howard
Donna Perry
Bill Popfinger
Andrew Filion
Sherry Cashman
Bunny Barasch
David Hershkowitz

Joe Ricco, Jr.
Mike Galante
Dawn Darish
Jeffrey Feinman
CeCe Levy
Bob Boni
Paige West
Marc Fontaine
Grace Myer
Sue Nolton
Steve Dunkel
Jimmy Marohn Sr.
Bonnie Insko
Frank Popfinger
June Hudson
Randy Lee
Sam McKee
Darienne Oaks
John Paton
Randy Perry
George Berkner
Tommy Insko
Brandon Filion
Mike Forte
Moira Fanning

References

Pro Quest
New York Times
Newsday
New York Daily News
United States Trotting Association
Roosevelt Raceway Publicity Dept.
CeCe Levy
Dean Hoffman
Huffington Post
Wikipedia
Bill Shannon Biographical Dictionary
Observer Reporter
Canadian Horse Racing Hall of Fame
Roosevelt Raceway Media Guide
The Harness Racing Museum and Hall of Fame

Index

CPSIA information can be obtained at www.ICGtesting.com
Printed in the USA
BVOW03s2144091214

378713BV00012B/85/P